A Practical Guide to Classroom-based Assessment in L2

신유선 지음

KM 경문사

Preface

This book is designed for educators, language assessment professionals, and learners in the field of language learning and assessment. It serves as a comprehensive guide for those interested in the practical aspects of designing, implementing, and interpreting assessments in L2 classrooms.

How This Book Is Structured Structured into three main parts, the book begins with a foundation in understanding language assessment, covering the purposes and types of assessments, and looking into the quality of assessments through reliability, validity, and fairness considerations. The second part focuses on developing assessment tools in the classroom, offering practical guidance on test specification, descriptive statistics, and scoring criteria. The final part assesses language ability across listening, reading, speaking, writing, grammar, and vocabulary, providing a holistic view of language proficiency assessment.

The book is divided into three main parts:

- **Understanding Language Assessment:** Explores the purpose, types, and quality of language assessments.
- **Developing Assessment Tools in the Classroom:** Guides the reader through the process of creating effective test specifications, understanding descriptive statistics, and developing scoring criteria.
- **Assessing Language Ability:** Focuses on practical approaches to assessing key language skills including listening, reading, speaking, writing, grammar, and vocabulary.

Teaching and Learning with This Book Each unit includes theoretical explanations, practical examples, and exercises designed to bridge the gap between theory and practice. The book also encourages active engagement with the content through reflective questions, application tasks, and case studies.

What's Special About This Book Unique to this guide is its focus on classroom-based assessment, emphasizing practicality and applicability. It offers a balance between theoretical insights and practical advice, enabling teachers and instructors to tailor their assessment practices to meet the diverse needs of their learners. Additionally, the book highlights the latest trends in language assessment, including dynamic and alternative assessments, fostering a more inclusive and effective learning environment. I hope this book serves as a valuable resource, guiding you through the complexities of language assessment and enriching your professional practice or academic studies.

Contents

PART I Understanding Language Assessment

UNIT 3. Quality of Assessment

PART II Developing Assessment Tools in the classroom

UNIT 4. Test Specification

UNIT 5. Descriptive Statistics

PART I

Understanding Language Assessment

UNIT 1.

Purpose of Assessment

Key Points

In this unit you will be able to:

1. Understand differences among measurement, testing, assessment, and evaluation
2. Understand the importance of assessment in L2 learning process
3. Learn about the major purposes of assessment: aptitude, diagnostic, placement, achievement, proficiency tests

Introduction of the Purpose of Assessment

This unit focuses on the significance of assessments in language learning, starting with the basics - differentiating between measurement, testing, assessment, and evaluation. It highlights the critical role assessments play in learning a second language (L2) and covers the key types of assessments: aptitude, diagnostic, placement, achievement, and proficiency. By defining and distinguishing these essential concepts, the introduction aims to provide a thorough understanding of how each assessment type aids in the educational journey, setting the groundwork for an in-depth look at their impact on language education.

What is Assessment: Measurement, Testing, Assessment, and Evaluation

Before moving on the various types of issues on language assessment, we need to differentiate four basic interrelated concepts: measurement, testing, assessment, and evaluation. In spite of important differences among these terms, these are often used exchangeably with assessment or even evaluation. **Measurement** refers to the process of quantifying observed performance, physical features, or traits. For example, a student's height can be measured in centimeters, while his level of 'anxiety might be quantified through tests assigning scores to specific traits. **Testing** involves the use of tools or methods intended to measure learners' abilities or knowledge in completing particular tasks. For instance, a language proficiency test assesses general language ability, while a quiz on the correct use of indefinite articles assesses specific grammar knowledge. Testing is only one form of assessment. Tests are arranged procedures that take place at specific times when the learners are performing at their best, knowing that their answers will be evaluated and measured (Brown, 2004, p. 4).

Meanwhile, **assessment** can be defined as the ongoing process of collecting information about learners' using different methods or tools such as tests, quizzes, or portfolios, etc. Assessment includes many informal and formal methods of evaluating learners' progress, educational needs, academic readiness or level of skill acquisition. Last, **evaluation**, according to Weiss (1972), is the systematic gathering of information for the purpose of making decisions. It is not intended to evaluate an individual's performance, but rather to gain a deeper understanding of the curriculum and make a judgment about it. In the process, we can decide the value of a course, an instruction, or even a whole curriculum. In this way, evaluation encompasses all aspects of the educational system.

Figure 1.1

Test, Measurement, Assessment, and Evaluation

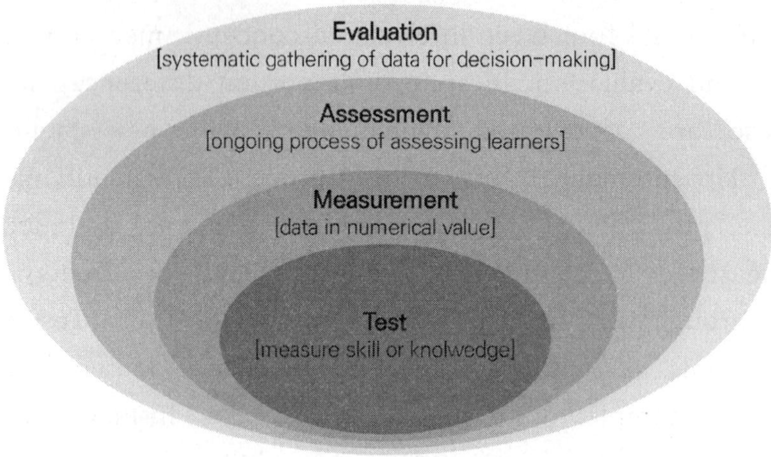

The Importance of Assessment in L2 Learning

In sum, as an umbrella term, assessment refers to all the activities carried out between teachers and learners, "which provide information to be used as feedback to modify the teaching and learning activities in which they are engaged" (Black & William, 1998, p. 2). Assessment activities include events, tools, processes, and decisions (Taylor & Nolen, 2008). Assessments are considered important because they motivate students to learn. With this understanding, teachers can use assessment strategies to influence learning outcomes. Assessment strategies focused on knowledge recall, for example, are likely to promote superficial learning. Conversely, if teachers select assessment strategies that encourage critical thinking or problem-solving, they will likely see higher levels of student performance in a given task. In addition, good assessment can encourage students to become more self-directed (Angelo & Cross, 1993). The purpose of assessment is not solely to motivate and self-direct learners. In addition to providing valuable feedback, assessments also contribute to ongoing quality improvement processes at the level of the course, lesson, and curriculum.

Assessment is a cornerstone of language learning, serving as a compass that guides both learners and educators through the intricate journey of acquiring a new language. Its role is essential, offering a comprehensive understanding of L2 learners' progress, strengths, and areas needing improvement. This significance spans various aspects of the learning process. Central to this role is the invaluable feedback assessment provides. Constructive feedback becomes a powerful tool as it helps students not only recognize their strengths and weaknesses but also empowers them to concentrate their efforts where improvement is required. Additionally, assessment contributes to the establishment of clear language learning goals and benchmarks, aligning learners' trajectories and motivating them towards their objectives. Regular evaluations then enable students to monitor their advancements, further fueling their determination to reach their targets.

The impact of assessment extends to educators who leverage assessment results to tailor instruction to individual needs. Armed with a deep understanding of each learner's proficiency level, teachers can skillfully adjust their strategies and materials, ensuring effective support for every learner. Moreover, assessments play a essential role in refining language learning curricula. Through careful analysis of assessment data, institutions identify trends and areas of challenge, facilitating nuanced curriculum adjustments that cater to specific learning requirements.

This standardized approach to assessment serves as a yardstick for measuring language proficiency, a crucial asset in academia and the professional world. The motivation derived from assessment fosters heightened engagement, propelling learners to actively participate in the learning process. Positive assessment outcomes improve self-confidence, sustaining a cycle of continuous effort. Furthermore, assessments drive learners to reflect on their learning paths, cultivating metacognitive skills that empower them to refine their strategies.

The sense of accountability nurtured by assessment extends to both learners and educators. Students embrace ownership of their learning experiences, while teachers embrace the responsibility to offer quality instruction, fostering growth. This practice in accountability enables learners to independently monitor their progress, fostering ongoing improvement beyond formal education. In today's interconnected global landscape, language proficiency is paramount for effective communication. Assessment ensures learners are equipped with the necessary skills for successful international interactions. Ultimately, assessment orchestrates a harmonious symphony of language acquisition, nurturing well-rounded linguistic competence, and enriching overall communication abilities.

Purpose of Assessment: Aptitude, Diagnostic, Placement, Achievement, and Proficiency Tests

Assessment instruments encompass a range of objectives, serving diverse purposes. Commercially developed tests have the potential to gauge proficiency, determine appropriate course placement, or pinpoint learners' strengths and weaknesses within linguistic categories. Meanwhile, classroom-based assessments can effectively diagnose learners' difficulties or measure achievements within specific units or courses. Explicitly outlining its purpose and objectives can be an essential initial step in the selection, design, revision, or adaptation of an assessment instrument. The categories of assessment instruments is generally framed within five primary types of language assessments: aptitude, diagnostic, placement, achievement, and proficiency tests. Each classification aligns with different aims, underlining the need for precision in determining the appropriate assessment approach for a given context.

Aptitude Tests

Aptitude refers to the ability to learn new things. Language aptitude tests is to assess a person's ability to learn new language skills. Since language aptitude tests are general in nature, they don't focus on a specific skill in a language. Rather, the tests measure a learner's ability to learn new language skills rapidly and effectively. Specifically, This test would evaluate the learner's ability to recognize phonetic differences, identify grammatical patterns, learn vocabulary, understand language rules, and analyze simple language texts. The results can help identify learners with a natural aptitude for language learning and may indicate their potential for success in second language acquisition.

Diagnostic Tests

The purpose of diagnostic tests is to determine a person's abilities in a certain field. Diagnostic tests are typically given at the beginning of a language learning course or program, as opposed to achievement and proficiency tests. The questions and tasks on a diagnostic test are typically outside the scope of the test-takers' abilities and their knowledge of the material. The results of the test show what one's strengths and weaknesses are in regard to language abilities. The results of a learner's diagnostic test can help teachers design lesson plans that address the learner's current skills gaps. Diagnostic tests can also be used to determine what areas learners need to improve upon to reach higher levels of proficiency. Diagnostic tests, in contrast to achievement tests, aim to reveal what learners need to know going forward. For example, a diagnostic test for English grammar might include questions on verb tenses, articles, and sentence structure.

Placement Tests

Placement tests serve to place students into a specific level of a language curriculum or program. Diagnostic tests and placement tests share some similarities. Placement tests are used as part of an educational process and are administered before a course or program of study is begun. Placement tests are used by teachers and administrators to group learners into classes according to their abilities. A placement test for English language classes may include questions on vocabulary, grammar, and listening comprehension. Based on the test results, the learner may be placed in a beginner, intermediate, or advanced level class, ensuring they are appropriately challenged and not overwhelmed.

Achievement Tests

An achievement test measures a learner's progress in learning a language and is typically graded. Unlike diagnostic, aptitude, and placement tests, achievement tests only cover the materials that learners should have already mastered during their studies. Achievement tests are used to assess whether learners have achieved course objectives and mastered appropriate knowledge and skills. In contrast to proficiency tests, achievement tests are directly related to language courses. Achievement tests are often summative because they are administered at the end of the semester. An achievement test for a English language course may include sections on vocabulary, reading comprehension, writing a short essay, and speaking tasks. The test is designed to evaluate how well the learner has grasped the language concepts taught during the course.

Proficiency Tests

The purpose of proficiency tests is to measure learners' proficiency in a language, regardless of how they learned the language or what level of competence they achieved. Such tests are designed to determine whether test-takers have reached a particular standard with respect to a set of abilities. The common feature of proficiency tests is that they do not rely on courses that test-takers may have taken previously. For some proficiency tests, "proficient" means having a sufficient command of the language for a specific purpose (Hughes, 2004). TOEFL, for instance, is used to determine whether a learner is proficient enough in English to pursue a degree program in the United States.

Proficiency tests serve as a gatekeeping function to decide if someone is accepted into a program. Most proficiency tests are norm-referenced and summative. The Test of English as a Foreign Language (TOEFL) is a proficiency test for English. It includes sections on listening comprehension, reading comprehension, speaking, and writing. The test evaluates a test taker's ability to use English in an academic context.

EXERCISES

Match the following terms with the correct definitions. Terms may be used more than once.

1. aptitude test	6. assessment
2. measurement	7. proficiency test
3. achievement test	8. numbers
4. diagnostic test	9. evaluation
5. test	10. placement test

1. A(n) ___________ is designed to measure strength, talent, or ability in a particular domain or area.
2. The process of gathering data and information about a person's performance, knowledge, skills, or abilities is called ___________.
3. A(n) ___________ is designed to identify a student's strengths and weaknesses in specific areas of knowledge or skills.
4. A(n) ___________ is used to determine the most appropriate educational program or level for a student based on their current abilities.
5. Assessment and ___________ are ongoing processes used to monitor progress and make decisions about instruction and learning.
6. A(n) ___________ measures a person's overall language proficiency in a specific language.
7. A(n) ___________ is a systematic procedure for measuring a sample of a person's behavior or performance in a specific domain.
8. ___________ is an essential component of the teaching and learning process, providing valuable feedback for improvement.

9. The primary purpose of a __________ is to assess what a student has learned or achieved after instruction.

10. A(n) __________ is typically used at the beginning of a language course to determine a student's language proficiency level.

11. Measurement involves assigning __________ to the observed characteristics or behaviors, allowing for quantitative comparisons.

12. The results of a __________ can help educators identify areas where a student may need additional support or intervention.

13. The process of assigning numbers or scores to represent the quantity of a characteristic or trait being assessed is known as __________.

14. A(n) __________ test is often used to assess language skills such as listening, speaking, reading, and writing.

15. A(n) __________ test is used to measure a student's performance in relation to specific learning goals or standards.

16. __________ involves the interpretation and analysis of assessment data to make judgments about a learner's performance or the effectiveness of a program.

UNIT 2.

Types of Language Assessment

Key Points

In this unit you will be able to:

1. Identify the types and characteristics of assessment: formative vs. summative, formal vs. informal, norm-referenced vs. criterion-referenced, discrete-point vs. integrative, direct vs. indirect testing
2. Classify and describe major characteristics of each assessment trend: traditional, alternative, and dynamic assessment

Introduction of the Types of Language Assessment

This unit focuses on the various types of language assessment which include formative vs. summative, formal vs. informal, norm-referenced vs. criterion-referenced, discrete-point vs. integrative, and direct vs. indirect testing. Additionally, the unit aims to classify and describe the major characteristics of each assessment trend, including traditional, alternative, and dynamic assessment methods. This introduction paves the way for an in-depth examination of language assessment's essential role in educational settings, underscoring the necessity of understanding these distinctions for accurately assessing learner progress and proficiency.

Types of Language Assessment

Assessment is a critical aspect of education and involves evaluating learners' learning progress, skills, and knowledge. Assessments can be categorized along various dimensions, and understanding these distinctions is valuable, as they often represent opposing poles in these terms (McAlpine, 2002).

Figure 2.1

Types of Assessment

Formative ↔	Summative
Informal ↔	Formal
Norm-referenced ↔	Criterion-referenced
Discrete-point ↔	Integrative
Direct ↔	Indirect

It's important to note that assessments can often fall into multiple categories simultaneously. For example, a final exam can be both summative (evaluating overall understanding) and criterion-referenced (measuring against specific learning objectives). Effective assessment practices consider the goals of the educational context and seek to provide a comprehensive understanding of students' progress and capabilities. Let's explore each category more extensively.

Formative vs. Summative Assessment

The purpose of formative assessment is to assist the learning process by providing feedback to the learner, which can be used to identify strengths and weaknesses and thus improve performance going forward. Formative assessments are integral during the learning process, providing ongoing feedback to students and educators about learning achievements and areas needing improvement. So, formative assessment emerges as the optimal approach when its outcomes are utilized by both students and instructors to facilitate the learning process. In contrast, summative assessment is primarily used to determine grading or readiness to progress. Summative assessment occurs typically at the end of a course and is meant to evaluate a student's overall performance. Summative assessment serves as a means to evaluate learners' abilities as well as to communicate their capabilities to external stakeholders, including administrators and employers.

Informal vs. Formal Assessment

Informal assessment is based on integrating judgments with other tasks, for example, marginal comments on papers, responses to essay drafts, advice about how to improve speaking ability, or suggestions about compensating for a reading difficulty. Most often, informal assessment is used to provide formative feedback. It tends to be less threatening, which leads to less stress for learners. Informal feedback, however, can be highly subjective or biased. Meanwhile, a formal assessment occurs when a student is aware that the task is being performed for assessment purposes, such as during a written test or performance assessment. Formal assessments are primarily summative in nature, and therefore, have a greater impact on a learner's motivation and cause an increased level of stress. As a result of their role in decision-making, formal assessments must meet higher standards of reliability and validity than informal assessments.

Norm-Referenced vs. Criterion-Referenced

The purpose of such tests is to rank learners based on their scores. Students are typically given a numerical score (such as 90 out of 100) and a percentile rank (such as 91 percent, which means that their score was higher than 91 percent of all test-takers, but lower than 9 percent on that test). A norm-referenced test interprets each student's score in terms of a mean, median, or standard deviation. Standardized tests like the Test of English for International Communication (TOEIC) or the Test of English as a Foreign Language (TOEFL) are examples of norm-referenced tests, designed to assess a large number of students, with results effectively disseminated to them. Criterion-referenced tests, by contrast, are designed to give students feedback on specific objectives of a lesson or course usually through grades. Criteria-referenced tests are typically classroom tests that are connected to the curriculum of the course. As long as the instrument measures the intended objectives, criteria-referenced tests do not have to account for the distribution of students' scores along a continuum.

Discrete-point vs. Integrative Tests

The arguments regarding discrete-point and integrative tests are rooted in two different teaching approaches: discrete-point tests date back to the days before communication was emphasized while integrative tests precisely correspond to communicative language teaching approaches (Plakans, 2013). In discrete-point tests, it is assumed that each component of a language can be broken down and tested independently. There are four components of language acquisition: listening, speaking, reading, and writing, as well as discrete units of language (phonology, graphology, morphology, lexicon, syntax, and discourse). It was claimed that a language proficiency test should cover all four skills and as many discrete linguistic points as possible. Students often struggle to understand how discrete-point tests contribute to language ability overall. As the field shifted towards emphasizing real communication and context, new approaches were sought. Oller (1979) argued that language skills are interconnected and can't be tested separately. He said that communicative skills are so interconnected that they can't be tested by just grammar or vocabulary tests. Others supported this idea, which led to "integrative testing".

Integrative tests aim to measure language skills in a holistic way. Two examples were *cloze tests* and *dictations*. A cloze test is an integrative language assessment tool where a passage is provided with certain words removed. Learners are required to fill in the blanks with appropriate words that fit the context, using their understanding of grammar, vocabulary, and discourse structure. The purpose of the cloze test is to assess both comprehension and the ability to predict missing information based on the surrounding text. Dictation is another integrative assessment technique where a speaker reads a passage aloud, and learners transcribe what they hear. This test evaluates listening, writing, and spelling skills simultaneously. Learners must understand spoken language, apply their knowledge of grammar and vocabulary, and produce an accurate written text.

Supporters claimed that they measured overall language proficiency. Cloze tests tapped into vocabulary, grammar, reading skills, and more. Dictations required listening, writing, and memory skills. Both were seen as integrative because they combined various language abilities. Initially, there was the idea that all these skills couldn't be separated, forming a "unitary trait hypothesis." The unitary trait hypothesis in the context of language testing refers to the theory that all language abilities can be attributed to a single underlying proficiency or competence. This hypothesis proposes that if someone is skilled in one language domain, they are likely to be skilled in others, because all language skills are manifestations of a single, unitary linguistic capability (Oller, 1979). This idea stands in contrast to the multiple competencies hypothesis, which suggests that language proficiency consists of distinct skills—such as reading, writing, speaking, and listening—that may develop at different rates and are not necessarily interdependent (Canale & Swain, 1980).

In practical terms, the unitary trait hypothesis would imply that a single test could effectively measure overall language proficiency, without needing to separately assess the different skills. However, this hypothesis is controversial and has been challenged by empirical research showing that language abilities can indeed be distinct and that proficiency in one area does not always correlate with proficiency in another (Bachman, 1990). This has led to a more refined understanding in language assessment, with tests often designed to evaluate specific skills rather than assuming a uniform proficiency across all areas of language use (Purpura, 1999).

Direct vs. Indirect Testing

In the context of language testing, direct and indirect testing are two different approaches used to assess language proficiency. Direct testing assesses the language skills by directly measuring the ability to perform in real-life language tasks. The test tasks closely resemble the actual language use that learners would encounter in authentic situations. Direct testing aims to evaluate learners' communicative competence by presenting them with real communicative tasks, such as engaging in conversations, writing emails, or completing role-plays. Advantages of direct testing include authenticity, as it provides a more authentic assessment of language skills, reflecting how language is used in real-life situations. Additionally, direct testing allows learners to demonstrate their ability to use language in meaningful contexts, making the assessment more relevant. Indirect testing, on the other hand, assesses language proficiency through discrete-point items that target specific language components, such as grammar, vocabulary, or reading comprehension. These items do not necessarily replicate real-life language use but focus on isolated language features. Advantages of indirect testing include its ability to provide a more detailed and specific evaluation of particular language aspects, making it suitable for diagnosing strengths and weaknesses in learners' language skills. Additionally, indirect tests are often objective and can be scored more easily becuase the responses are discrete.

Hughes (1990) supports the use of both direct and indirect testing methods. He emphasizes the importance of employing a variety of test formats and task types to assess different language skills comprehensively. A balanced approach that includes both direct and indirect testing allows for a more holistic evaluation of learners' language abilities, providing a broader perspective on their overall language proficiency. The choice between direct and indirect testing depends on the specific testing goals, the target language skills being assessed, and the context in which the assessment takes place. A well-designed language test may incorporate elements of both direct and indirect testing to provide a comprehensive and accurate evaluation of learners' language proficiency.

Trends of Traditional, Alternative, and Dynamic Assessment

The relationship among traditional, alternative, and dynamic assessment in L2 language testing is complex and interconnected. These assessment approaches represent different paradigms for evaluating language learners, each with its own principles and methods. Let's explore the relationship among these three approaches:

Traditional Assessment

Traditional assessment refers to the conventional methods of evaluating students' knowledge and skills, often focusing on rote memorization and discrete content knowledge. The primary goal of traditional assessment is to measure a student's ability to recall specific information and apply predefined procedures. Traditional assessment focuses on evaluating discrete language components and content knowledge. It often employs standardized tests with closed-ended questions to measure learners' knowledge of grammar, vocabulary, and reading comprehension. While traditional assessment is efficient for large-scale testing and provides a standardized benchmark, it may not fully capture learners' real-world language use, critical thinking, or communication skills. These assessments are typically standardized, using closed-ended questions and predetermined formats. Common types of traditional assessments include multiple-choice exams, fill-in-the-blank questions, and true/false tests. The assessment process prioritizes objectivity and efficiency, making it suitable for large-scale testing scenarios. The purpose of traditional assessment is to rank students based on their performance, determine grades, and provide accountability metrics for educational institutions.

Influencing Theories: Behavioral Psychology, Structural Linguistics, and Psychometric Structuralism

Traditional assessment draws upon the principles of behavioral psychology, which emphasizes observable behaviors and responses to stimuli (Skinner, 1957). In the context of language assessment, this approach focuses on assessing discrete language elements and rote memorization. Characteristics of traditional assessment influenced by behavioral psychology include standardized tests with closed-ended questions that measure specific language knowledge and skills. These tests often involve tasks like multiple-choice questions and fill-in-the-blank exercises. The goal is to assess whether learners can recall and reproduce language components they have learned.

Structural linguistics has also significantly shaped traditional assessment characteristics. This linguistic approach focuses on analyzing the formal structure of language, including syntax, morphology, phonology or etc. (Chomsky, 1957). In line with this perspective, traditional assessments design questions that target isolated language components. For instance, grammar exercises, sentence parsing tasks, and vocabulary matching exercises reflect the influence of structural linguistics. The aim is to assess learners' understanding of language rules and structures in isolation.

Psychometric structuralism, a branch of psychology that deals with the measurement of psychological traits, contributes to the characteristics of traditional assessment. It emphasizes the use of reliable and valid measurement tools to assess cognitive abilities. Traditional language assessments are designed to meet psychometric criteria by using standardized formats and established testing procedures. These tests aim to provide consistent and objective measurements of learners' language proficiency. The focus on quantifiable results and objective scoring aligns with the principles of psychometric structuralism (Weir, 2005).

Alternative Assessment

In our society where everything, even education, is mass-produced, tests have gained a reputation for being foolproof. People desire tests for everything, especially if they're quick, affordable, and give instant results. But research and experience during the 1990s challenged the idea that all skills and individuals could be measured using traditional tests. This led to the rise of alternative assessment. When teachers and students realized the limitations of standardized tests, they looked for alternatives. They proposed using various methods like portfolios, journals, observations, self-assessments, and peer assessments to gather a range of information about students. Some saw these alternatives as ethical, promoting fairness and a balanced classroom dynamics. Others presented evidence that such alternatives, like those focusing on ongoing progress (formative assessment), were more effective (Lynch & Shaw, 2005; Ross, 2005). These assessments promote critical thinking, creativity, and the ability to synthesize information.

Alternative assessment seeks to assess not only what students know, but how well they can apply that knowledge to solve complex problems. Thus, the purpose of alternative assessment goes beyond assigning grades; it aims to provide a more comprehensive view of students' learning progress. By assessing skills such as communication, teamwork, and research, alternative assessment nurtures lifelong learning skills crucial for success in a dynamic world. Moreover, alternative assessment is inherently more inclusive, accommodating diverse learning styles and allowing students to demonstrate their understanding in ways that suit their strengths. In fact, drawing a strict line between what's seen as traditional and alternative assessment isn't straightforward. Many assessment forms fall somewhere in between or even combine aspects of both approaches. As Armstrong (1994) and Bailey (1998) highlighted, we should appreciate and use the assessment methods available to us for their unique purposes. However, it's also important to consider whether we can apply the concepts on the right side of the list in our classrooms.

Influencing Theories on Alternative Assessment: CLT

Communicative Language Teaching (CLT) has significantly shaped the landscape of alternative assessment within the realm of language education. With a focus on communication as the ultimate objective of language learning, CLT's impact has extended to the design and administration of alternative assessment methods (Brown & Abeywickrama, 2019; Littleword, 1981; Savignon, 1997). This pedagogical approach underscores the necessity of enabling learners to utilize language authentically in real-life contexts, thereby influencing the structure of alternative assessments. Furthermore, CLT underscores the teaching of practical language functions like persuasion, description, narration, and requests. Alternative assessments influenced by CLT focus on assessing learners' ability to perform these language functions rather than simply testing isolated vocabulary or grammar. This might entail tasks such as engaging in negotiations, delivering persuasive speeches, or participating in collaborative problem-solving tasks.

CLT also recognizes the interconnectedness of language skills and advocates for their simultaneous teaching and assessment. Consequently, CLT-influenced alternative assessments incorporate tasks demanding the integration of multiple skills. For instance, a comprehensive project could entail researching a topic (reading), presenting findings (speaking), and composing a written report (writing). The emphasis on contextual learning endorsed by CLT is seamlessly integrated into alternative assessments. Alternative assessments inspired by CLT provide learners with a purpose for using language, simulating real communication situations. This ensures that learners not only demonstrate language proficiency but also their ability to adapt their language use to different contexts.

Another tenet of CLT is interactive and collaborative learning. Consequently, alternative assessments aligned with CLT frequently involve tasks necessitating peer interaction and cooperative endeavors. Group projects, role-plays, debates, and discussions are common examples of these assessment activities. These tasks measure not only individual language competencies but also the capacity to engage in meaningful discourse with others. To summarize, the impact of CLT on alternative assessment is distinguished by its emphasis on authenticity, real-world application, language functions, skill integration, contextualization, and interactive communication. These principles ensure that alternative assessments harmonize with the communicative objectives of language education, prioritizing learners' efficacy in utilizing language for communication and practical contexts.

Dynamic Assessment

Dynamic assessment stands out as a language assessment approach that highlights the active, interactive way we acquire and learn languages. Dynamic assessment is rooted in the Zone of Proximal Development (ZPD) theory and Vygotsky's socio-cultural framework. It views assessment as an instructional tool, using interactive tasks to gauge learners' learning potential and capacity for improvement. Dynamic assessment involves scaffolding, where the assessor provides guidance and support to learners during assessment tasks. This approach emphasizes learners' ability to learn and adapt, providing insights into their learning trajectory and potential for growth.

This method has gained significance in today's language classrooms for various reasons. Instead of just focusing on the end results, dynamic assessment gives more importance to how language skills develop over time. This enables language teachers to monitor the progress their students are making and adjust their teaching methods accordingly. By using dynamic assessment, language teachers can tailor their teaching to match the specific needs and abilities of each learner. Through consistent assessment of language development, teachers can spot areas where students need extra help and offer feedback that can help them progress faster.

Moreover, dynamic assessment urges students to take a more involved role in their language learning. It prompts them to think about their own language development and identify areas where they can get better. This approach boosts motivation and interest in the language classroom. Dynamic assessment paints a truer picture of a learner's language skills by considering both their pace of improvement and the process of language growth. This information aids teachers in deciding where to place students in language classes and provides more meaningful feedback. Furthermore, dynamic assessment lets language teachers offer customized feedback and instruction that takes into account each learner's individual strengths and weaknesses. This personalized approach fosters more effective and efficient language learning. Despite its numerous advantages, dynamic assessment faces several significant challenges. A primary concern is its resource intensity; it requires assessors who are not only adept in assessment techniques but also effective as educators, capable of providing immediate and relevant feedback and interventions. This dual role necessitates a substantial investment of time and effort from both assessors and learners, making dynamic assessment less practical for large groups or routine assessments where resources are scarce.

Another challenge arises from the highly interactive and tailored nature of dynamic assessment, which complicates standardization and reliability. Because the assessment is customized based on each learner's responses, ensuring consistency across different assessors and learners is difficult. This variability can affect the reliability and fairness of the assessment, making it challenging to compare results across different contexts or among various individuals. Furthermore, due to its interactive nature, dynamic assessment is inherently time-consuming. This can make it impractical in educational settings where time is limited, such as during regular classroom hours or in large-scale testing situations.

Despite these challenges, dynamic assessment remains a valuable tool in educational contexts, especially for understanding a learner's potential and learning processes. It is frequently used alongside more traditional forms of assessment to provide a more accurate of a learner's abilities, underscoring its utility despite the aforementioned drawbacks.

Influencing Theories on Dynamic Assessment: Vygotsky's Theory and ZPD

Dynamic assessment is grounded in the sociocultural theory of Vygotsky, particularly the concept of the Zone of Proximal Development (ZPD) (Vygotsky, 1978). This approach emphasizes the importance of social interaction, guided assistance, and the potential for cognitive growth through collaboration. Dynamic assessment aims to understand learners' developmental potential and provide targeted support to help them achieve higher levels of performance.

The central idea of dynamic assessment is to assess not only what learners can currently do on their own but also what they can achieve with the right guidance. It focuses on learners' potential for cognitive development, allowing them to demonstrate skills and knowledge that might not be apparent through traditional testing (Lidz, 1991). Dynamic assessment involves interaction between the assessor and the learner. This interaction is characterized by guided assistance, where the assessor provides support, hints, and scaffolding to help the learner perform tasks that might be slightly beyond their current independent capabilities (Poehner & Lantolf, 2005). Assessment tasks are designed to challenge learners within their ZPD— Figure 2.1 ZPD and Scaffolding the gap between what they can do on their own and what they can do with support. These tasks are carefully scaffolded, meaning that the level of difficulty is adjusted based on the learner's responses. The goal is to push learners slightly beyond their current level while providing the necessary assistance for success. Dynamic assessment often involves problem-solving tasks that require learners to think critically and apply their knowledge in novel situations. These tasks encourage collaboration between the assessor and the learner, allowing them to work together to reach solutions.

Relationships among Three Assessment Approaches

While these assessment approaches differ in their methods and underlying philosophies, they can be integrated to provide a more comprehensive understanding of learners' language abilities. Alternative assessment can be seen as a bridge between traditional and dynamic assessment. It shares elements of authenticity and real-world application with dynamic assessment's focus on potential development. Integrating dynamic assessment principles into both traditional and alternative assessment can enhance the effectiveness of the assessment process by considering learners' ZPD and providing tailored support.

In practice, a balanced approach that draws on all three assessment types can offer a holistic evaluation of learners' language skills. This might involve combining traditional tests to measure foundational knowledge, alternative tasks to assess application and critical thinking, and dynamic assessment strategies to uncover learners' potential and capacity for improvement. This integrative approach acknowledges the complexity of language learning and provides a richer picture of learners' language proficiency and development.

Table 2.1

Differences among Traditional Assessment, Alternative Assessment, and Dynamic Assessment

Aspect	Traditional Assessment	Alternative Assessment	Dynamic Assessment
Theoretical Foundations	Behavioral Psychology Structural Linguistics Psychometric Structuralism	Communicative Language teaching (CLT)	Sociocultural theory Vygotsky' s Zone Proximal Development
Characteristics	Structured, standardized, typically pen-and-paper format	More flexible, diverse, and authentic tasks	Interactive, individualized, focused on learning process
Distinctive Features	Emphasis on reliability and objectivity	Focus on real-world application and contextual learning	Assesses potential for cognitive growth and learning
Types	Multiple-choice, true/false, short answer, etc.	Portfolios, projects, performances, peer assessments	Scaffolding techniques, problem-solving tasks
Interpretation of Scores	Often quantitative, rank-based (percentiles, grades)	Qualitative, holistic, emphasis on mastery and growth	Qualitative, emphasizes process, ZPD
Question Types	Primarily recall and recognition questions	Open-ended, application-based, reflective questions	Prompts that guide problem-solving and critical thinking
Purpose	Summative, measure final outcomes	Formative, assess learning progress and understanding	Formative, identify learning potential and barriers
Focus	Product-oriented, assesses end results	Process-oriented, values learning and understanding	Interaction-oriented, assesses learning process

Table 2.2

Strengths and Weaknesses of the Three Assessment Types

	Traditional Assessment
Strengths	**Objectivity:** tend to provide consistent and objective results with their standardized formats and clear criteria.
	Efficiency: often more time-efficient to administer and score, especially in large-scale testing situations
	Focused Content: can effectively evaluate specific language elements, allowing for targeted evaluation of language skills.
	Established Standards: often have established norms and benchmarks, making it easier to compare learners' performance against established standards.
Weaknesses	**Lack of Authenticity:** often focus on discrete language elements and isolated skills, which may not reflect real-life language use and communication functions.
	Limited Application: may not effectively measure learners' ability to use language in practical contexts.
	Narrow Assessment Scope: may not capture the full range of learners' language abilities, as they tend to emphasize specific skill areas such as grammar, reading, or vocabulary
	Inadequate Feedback: may provide limited feedback that doesn't offer insights into learners' overall language development.

	Alternative Assessment
Strengths	**Authenticity:** reflect real-world language use, allowing learners to demonstrate their ability to communicate meaningfully in practical situations.
	Holistic Evaluation: provide a more comprehensive view of language proficiency by assessing their ability to integrate multiple language skills.
	Higher Engagement: The interactive and creative nature can engage learners more effectively, leading to increased motivation.
	Diverse Assessment: offer a wider range of task types, accommodating various learning styles and preferences, promoting inclusivity.
Weaknesses	**Subjectivity:** often involve open-ended tasks and authentic performance, can introduce subjectivity in scoring and interpretation.
	Complex Scoring: can be time-consuming and challenging due to the diversity of responsesm, leading to inconsistencies in scoring and difficulties in establishing grading criteria.
	Validity Concerns: Ensuring the validity and reliability can be challenging, especially if the tasks are not well-aligned with specific learning objectives.
	Limited Generalizability: often evaluate learners' performance in specific tasks which might not accurately predict their language proficiency in different situations.

	Dynamic Assessment
Strengths	**Individualized Support:** offers personalized guidance and scaffolding, allowing assessors to understand learners' potential and provide targeted support.
	Developmental Insight: assessors gain insights into learners' ability to benefit from instruction and adapt their learning strategies, fostering cognitive growth.
	Flexible Assessment: assessment tasks can be adjusted based on learners' responses, ensuring that learners are challenged appropriately and receive tailored feedback.
	Transferable Skills: focuses on learners' potential for development, fostering skills that go beyond the specific assessment task and can be applied to other contexts.
Weaknesses	**Time and Resource Intensive:** requires more time and resources compared to traditional or alternative assessments
	Scoring Complexity: can be complex, as it involves assessing both the learner's initial performance and their response to guidance and scaffolding.
	Reliability Concerns: The consistency of scoring results may be compromised due to the variability in the level of guidance.
	Limited Standardization: often tailored to individual learners, making it challenging to standardize the assessment process.

EXERCISES

Match the following terms with the correct definitions. Terms may be used more than once.

1. traditional assessment	7. norm-referenced test
2. alternative assessment	8. criterion-referenced test
3. summative assessment	9. integrative testing
4. formative assessment	10. cloze test
5. authentic	11. portfolio
6. dynamic assessment	

1. __________ focuses on authentic approaches that allow students to demonstrate their understanding through real-life tasks and projects.

2. Grading in traditional assessment is typically __________, providing a single score that may not capture the full picture of a student's abilities.

3. A __________ is influenced by Vygotskian theories, which emphasize learning potential and the role of scaffolding in cognitive development.

4. A __________ evaluates a learner's performance based on predefined criteria or standards.

5. __________ assessment is conducted at the end of a course or unit to evaluate learners' overall performance and assign a final grade.

6. __________ involves ongoing evaluation and feedback throughout the learning process to support learners' progress and development.

7. In alternative assessment, student performance is often assessed through __________ tasks, presentations, or portfolios.

8. A __________ compares a learner' performance to the performance of other test-takers to determine their relative standing.

9. __________ methods aim to evaluate a student's ability to combine multiple language skills, such as listening, reading, speaking, and writing.

10. A __________ often includes a passage where words have been omitted, requiring students to use their knowledge of grammar and vocabulary to complete the text.

11. __________ methods, influenced by CLT-related theories, emphasize authentic tasks and real-world applications to measure a student's practical skills.

12. A teacher collects class work, quizzes, book reports, and writing assignments to determine students' strengths and weaknesses in an L2 language class. This is known as __________.

UNIT 3.

Quality of Assessment

Key Points

In this unit you will be able to:

1. Understand the major quality concepts of language assessment: reliability, validity, authenticity, practicality, authenticity, and fairness
2. Analyze the relationship between reliability and validity
3. Define the correlation in the language testing

Introduction to Quality of Assessment

This unit covers the criteria for selecting effective assessment tools, guided by five fundamental qualities essential to language assessment: reliability, validity, authenticity, practicality, and fairness. It's imperative for assessment methods within educational settings to provide accurate and reliable information, as interpretations and decisions are frequently based on test data. A comprehensive understanding of reliability and validity is indispensable for educators to assess the accuracy, dependability, and credibility of assessment tools.

Reliability Issues

Reliability is a critical aspect of language testing that refers to the consistency and stability of test scores over repeated administrations or among different raters. A test is deemed reliable if it consistently yields similar results under comparable conditions. Conversely, unreliable outcomes can distort our understanding of a learner's language proficiency. Ensuring reliability involves the test providing consistent scores for the same individual upon repeated administrations, highlighting the importance of test design and administration. It is important for teachers to know that some level of error will be present during the administration of tests. Teachers can select a test tool with a low estimate of error and a high degree of reliability by using statistical methods. A learner's illness, fatigue, anxiety, or testing strategy can lead to a student-related issue in reliability. Test administration-related issues many result from the conditions of the test administration, including noise outside of the classroom, photocopy of the test, lights in the classroom, or weather, *etc.* Last, test reliability is related to the nature of the test itself.

Reliability stands as an essential aspect of language testing, signifying the stability and consistency of test scores across repeated administrations or among diverse raters. A test is deemed reliable when it generates uniform outcomes under similar circumstances, while unreliable results can ensue in misleading interpretations of learners' language prowess. To attain reliability, a test must yield consistent scores for the same student upon multiple occasions, and it must consistently measure a specific language skill across its various items.

Teachers should be cognizant that a certain degree of error is inherent in test administration. However, the selection of a test tool with minimal estimated error and a high degree of reliability can be facilitated through the application of statistical techniques. Since assessment is used to form the basis of teaching, teachers should select the most technically appropriate instrument. There are many factors that influence test reliability, including student-related reliability, rater reliability, test administration reliability, and test reliability (Mousavi, 2002). Diverse elements, including a learner's health, fatigue, anxiety, or testing approach, can introduce student-related reliability issues. Test administration-related concerns may arise from the test-taking environment, encompassing external noise, photocopying complications, lighting conditions, or even weather disturbances. Lastly, the reliability of a test is intrinsically tied to its inherent nature and structure.

Rater Reliability

As part of the scoring process, rater reliability encompasses human raters' bias, or their subjectivity in assessing learners' written or spoken performance. There are two types of rater reliability: interrater reliability and intrarater reliability. **Interrater Reliability** refers to the degree of agreement or consistency between two or more raters in their scoring. In language assessment, this means that different assessors (teachers, examiners, or raters) give similar scores to the same language performance or response (Bachman, 2004). It is crucial for ensuring that the assessment of language skills is objective and not overly dependent on the subjective judgment of a single rater. Techniques such as the use of detailed scoring rubrics, extensive rater training, and regular calibration sessions are often employed to enhance interrater reliability (Weigle, 2002). Statistical measures such as Cohen's kappa are used to quantify the level of interrater reliability, providing a numerical value that indicates how much consensus there is among raters (Hallgren, 2012). Conversely, **intrarater reliability** refers to the consistency of ratings given by the same rater on different occasions. In the context of language assessment, this pertains to the ability of a single rater to maintain consistent scoring across different assessments of the same or similar tasks by the same individual or across different individuals (Knoch, 2009). Intrarater reliability addresses the issue of whether a rater's judgments are stable over time or if they are influenced by external factors such as mood, fatigue, or "halo effect." Enhancing intrarater reliability involves training raters to apply scoring criteria consistently and ensuring that they are aware of potential biases that may affect their scoring. Both interrater and intrarater reliability are foundational to the validity of language assessments. They ensure that the assessment process is fair, objective, and capable of producing reliable results that accurately reflect the language abilities of the test-takers. High levels of interrater and intrarater reliability contribute to the overall credibility and effectiveness of language testing and assessment systems.

◤ How to Improve Rater Reliability ◢

- Provide detailed scoring criteria and a detailed scoring key
- Train raters to produce consistent scores
- Identify acceptable responses and appropriate scores before scoring
- Identify test-takers by number, not by name
- Apply multiple and independent scoring

Test Reliability

In a vocabulary test, if a student takes the same test on two separate occasions and receives significantly different scores each time, the test lacks test-retest reliability. This inconsistency could be attributed to various factors, such as mood, fatigue, or environmental conditions, rather than indicating a genuine change in the student's vocabulary knowledge. Notably, test reliability can be influenced by the inherent nature of the test itself.

Similarly, when a test is too concise, learners may struggle to fully demonstrate their knowledge or skills. Conversely, an overly lengthy test can lead to fatigue towards its conclusion, affecting their performance. Moreover, poorly constructed test items can further impede learners' ability to excel on assessments. For instance, if items designed to measure the same reading skill yield inconsistent results for different subsets of items within a reading test, the test lacks internal consistency reliability. Such instances raise concerns that the test does not consistently measure the reading skill across all its items. Hence, the development of reliable test items is of paramount importance. Consequently, the question arises: how can classroom teachers create test items that ensure reliability? In this regard, there are valuable suggestions on how to craft reliable test items, as proposed by Hughes (2004). As a rule, adding more questions to a test that measures the same trait or attribute can increase the test's reliability.

How to Make Tests More Reliable

- Obtain enough samples for each knowledge or skill you intend to measure.
- Discard items that cannot accurately differentiate weaker from

stronger students.

- Develop items that are clear and unambiguous.
- Provide clear and explicit instructions during a test.
- Ensure that tests are well structured and readable.
- Make sure learners are familiar with the test format and techniques.

Activity: Potential reliability issues

Context An English language proficiency test, widely used in a language learning center, has shown inconsistent results for students retaking the test under similar conditions. For instance, a student, Jiho scored significantly higher on the speaking test during the first attempt but showed a marked decrease in the score in a subsequent attempt just a month later without any significant change in English language exposure. Such variability in test scores has raised concerns about the test's reliability.

Identify potential reliability issues affecting the test's consistency and propose targeted improvements to enhance the test's reliability and fairness.

Validity Issues

Validity is a fundamental concern in language testing, focusing on whether an assessment genuinely measures what it intends to measure. A valid test accurately reflects learners' language abilities, ensuring that the interpretations and decisions made based on test scores are meaningful and justified. A test is considered valid when it measures what is intended to be measured (Hughes, 1989; McCall, 1922). Assessments should accurately represent relevant features of the test-taker's knowledge, skills, or abilities if they closely correspond to the steps native language users undergo when performing tasks in real life.

Validity does not mean repeatable and dependable results, but instead means results that are good enough for the intended use. Does the test actually measure what it claims to measure? If a teacher wants to assess learners' grammar knowledge in his class, will the test provide grammar knowledge, will the test provide him with a valid indication of the learners' grammar knowledge? There are a number of methods that can be used to determine whether the test measures what the test developers intended it to measure. It is important for teachers to consider validity information carefully before selecting a test.

Validity, however, is not a binary yes or no kind of distinction, but rather viewed as a matter of degree. An inference may be more valid for one type of decision or for one group of test-takers than for another. As a result, when evidence indicates that the results of a test are sufficiently valid to support a decision about a specific group of test-takers on a particular occasion, we cannot simply assume that they will be equally valid in support of decisions about different groups or decisions taken on other occasions. Validation refers to the process of collecting evidence to support inferences based on the results of the test. There are several forms of validity such as *construct-related*, *content-related* validity, *criterion-related* validity, and *consequential* validity. Addressing validity concerns involves conducting thorough test development, using a variety of validation methods, and continually evaluating the alignment between the test's content, format, and its intended purpose. Ensuring validity is crucial for making informed decisions based on test results and promoting fairness and accuracy in language assessment.

Construct-related Validity

It may be difficult to establish construct validity for a new test than any type of validity. A construct refers to any underlying ability, attribute, or theoretical characteristic. A construct must be clearly defined in order to establish construct validity. Construct validity is difficult to measure because constructs are hypothetical and may even appear invisible. A learner's skills, abilities, and knowledge cannot be measured as directly as a learner's height or weight. In this way, an ability is not directly observable or measurable, but its results can be seen through performance in speaking or writing.

Bachman and Palmer (2010) suggested that test developers should define language ability in ways that are appropriate for each assessment situation. Language-related constructs need to be defined depending on the purpose of the assessment. They could range from broad categories such as 'overall language proficiency' or 'reading comprehension' to more specific questions about their own lives or the lives of their friends (Council of Europe, 2001). *Communication competence* or *proficiency* are linguistic constructs, while *self-efficacy* or *anxiety* can be psychological constructs. Different kinds of validity evidence can be used to determine the value of testing results.

Let's imagine, for example, you need to conduct an oral interview with students as part of performance assessment. Scores are assigned based on several factors, including fluency, grammatical accuracy, appropriate vocabulary use, pronunciation, etc. These factors are supported by a theoretical construct that describes them as essential components of speaking competence. The construct validity of the test could be in doubt if you only assessed pronunciation and grammar. Similarly, let's say you have created a simple grammar quiz, which covers the content of a recent unit and asks students to select the correct response. The quiz that you developed may be an adequate assessment of what was covered. But if the unit's goal is communicative use of grammar, then the grammar quiz fails to meet that goal.

Communicative Language Ability (Competence)

In language testing and assessment, many researchers have evolved a model called communicative language ability or communicative competence. As a result, terminology has become confusing (Celce-Murcia et al., 1995; McNamara, 1996) because the terms 'model' and 'framework' are used with a range of different meanings in a testing context. The term 'construct' is used to describe the components of the model in this section.

Canale and Swain (1980) provided the first model of what they called 'communicative competence.' The authors argued that communicative competence is defined as the interaction between grammatical skills, or knowledge of grammar, and sociolinguistic skills, or knowledge of how languages are used. In their view, communicative competence differs from communicative performance, which refers to language use in communication situations. They also suggested that tests or assessments must address both communicative competence aspects (grammatical and sociolinguistic competence) by incorporating tasks that demand communicative performance.

Canale and Swain (1980)' model identified four components of communicative competence:

1. Grammatical competence: the ability to recognize the grammatical rules of a language (vocabulary, pronunciation, spelling, etc.).
2. Sociolinguistic competence: mastery of the codes of language use in a specific context (applying appropriate vocabulary, register, politeness, and style).

3. Discourse competence: the ability to combine language structures in a variety of cohesive forms (such as political speeches, poetry).
4. Strategic competence: the use of verbal and nonverbal communication strategies to enhance communication efficiency and, where necessary, to solve problems that arise when communication breakdowns occur.

Figure 3.1

Canale and Swain (1980)'s Model of Communicative Competence

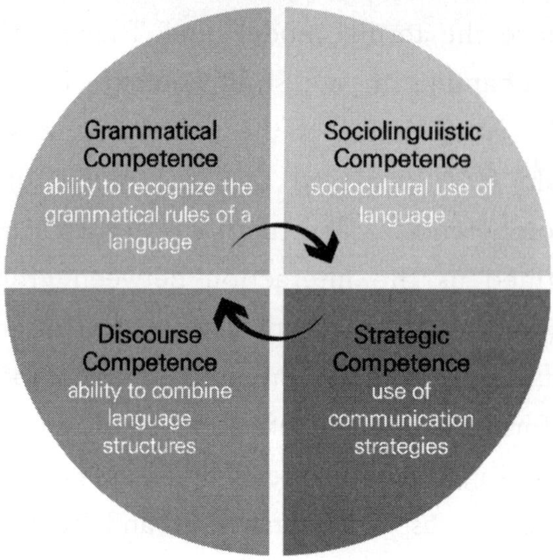

Bachman's (1990) model of communicative language ability consisted of four components: organizational competence (grammatical competence and textual competence) and pragmatic competence (illocutionary competence and sociolinguistic competence). Discourse competence is divided into two elements: cohesion and coherence. Cohesion falls under textual competence, but coherence is integrated into illocutionary competence. The left-hand branch of the tree represents the formal aspects of language usage, including grammatical competence and textual competence. This refers to the ability to recognize the way texts (spoken or written) are organized in a way that makes them conventional for listeners or readers. Right-hand side of the tree is now known as pragmatic competence, which is defined as the ability to utilize language in a specific context and the rules for doing so. Hence, pragmatic competence has been divided into two parts. Language functions and speech acts constitute illocutionary competence, as described by Halliday (1973) and Austin (1962).

Figure 3.2

Components of Language Competence (Bachman, 1999, p. 87)

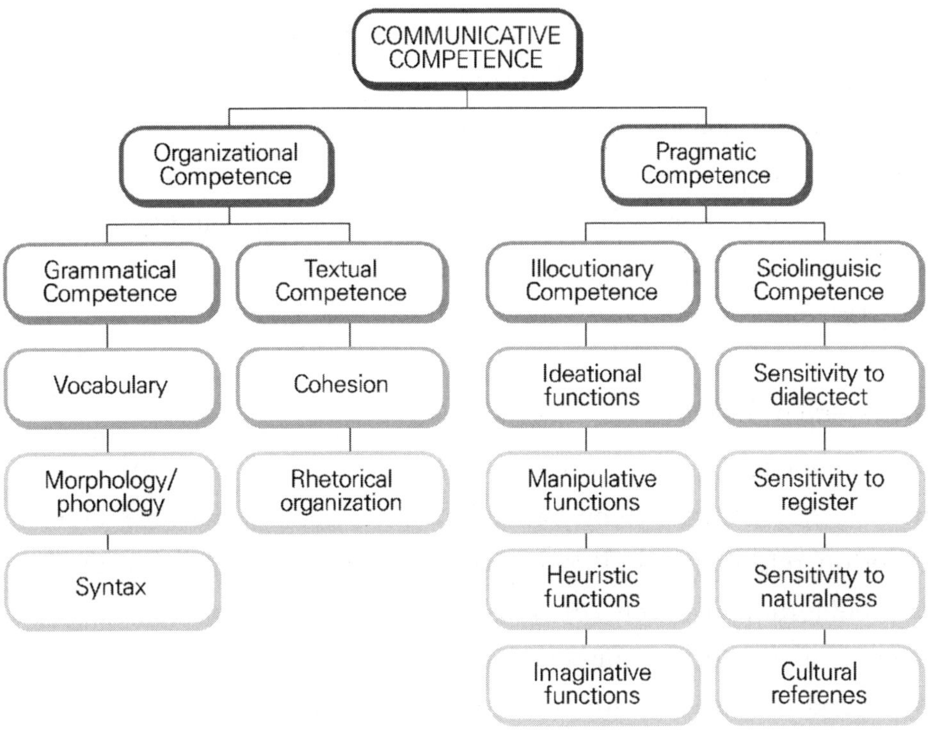

Content-related Validity

Content-related validity is assumed when a test or subtest reflects a particular content which was intended to be covered. If a test is going to have good content validity, it must contain the content in a representative manner. For example, an achievement test that has only 10 grammar and vocabulary definition questions has not adequately represented the content of the language domain. There should be several items representative of each domain, level, and skill in a good representation of the content.

It is unlikely that a test will be accurate if major areas outlined in the specification are underrepresented. Such a test is likely to have a harmful backwash effect. Untested areas are likely to be neglected by teachers and learners. Test content is often determined by what's easy to test rather than what's important (Hughes, 2004). A good way to prevent this is to write complete test specifications and make sure that the test content is a fair representation of them. Therefore, content-related validity should take place during the development of a test, not after it is already being used (Hughes, 2004).

Criterion-related Validity

Criterion-related validity is referred to the extent to which the "criterion" of the test has actually been reached. Most classroom-based assessments are criterion-referenced and designed by teachers. Students are expected to meet predetermined levels of performance on such tests, and 80% is considered a minimum passing grade. Criteria-related validity is best demonstrated through a comparison of test results to other measures of the same criterion. In case the student is required to read topic-related materials and answer the questions for a course unit test, the student's test results may be compared to a commercially available test that measures the same reading ability. A classroom test designed to assess mastery of a grammatical feature in communicative use will have criterion-related validity if test scores are corroborated either by observed following performance or by other communicative indicators.

There are usually two types of criterion-related validity: *concurrent* and *predictive* validity. A test has concurrent validity if the results of the test are supported by other concurrent performance. A high score on a language course, for example, will only be valid if it is supported by actual proficiency in the language. Predictive validity is relevant to placement tests, or achievement tests whose purpose is to determine the readiness of students to move on to the next level. In such cases, the test is designed to predict whether a student will succeed in the future, not to measure concurrent abilities.

Consequential Validity

Consequential validity includes all the consequences of a test, including its accuracy in measuring intended criteria, its impact on preparing learners, and its intended or unintended social consequences. Researches (Bachman & Palmer, 2010; Cheng, 2008b; Choi, 2008; Davies, 2003; Taylor, 2005) used the term "impact" for consequential validity, perhaps embracing more broadly the many consequences of assessment, before and after the test. The impact of testing and the use of test scores can be viewed at a macro level on society and education systems and at a micro level on individual test-takers.

In language assessment, consequential validity is also known as washback, or "the effect of testing on teaching and learning" (Hughes, 2004, p. 1). Messick (1996) emphasized the fact that washback may both promote and inhibit learning, highlighting the concept of beneficial and harmful washback. *Beneficial washback* refers to the positive impact that a test has on teaching and learning practices. When a test effectively aligns with desired learning outcomes, it can enhance teaching methods and encourage learners to focus on meaningful language use. Teachers often tailor their instruction to match the skills and content assessed in the test, leading to more relevant and engaging lessons. Learners, in turn, invest effort in acquiring the language skills required for success on the test, which can ultimately lead to improved language proficiency.

Harmful washback occurs when a test distorts teaching and learning practices in ways that hinder the development of meaningful language skills. For instance, if a test places excessive emphasis on rote memorization or test-specific strategies, teachers might prioritize these aspects over authentic language use. Learners may resort to memorizing answers instead of understanding the language's nuances, leading to superficial language proficiency. A test that provides beneficial washback is one that positively influences teaching and learning practices, enhancing language development and promoting meaningful skills.

How to Make a Test Valid

- Ensure that a test's objectives are well-defined, specific, and aligned with the language skills you intend to assess.
- Make sure that the test content accurately represents the language skills being evaluated.
- Ensure that the test measures what it's intended to measure by aligning the test items with the theoretical constructs of language proficiency.
- Include a diverse range of tasks that address different language skills, such as reading, listening, oral, and written expression.

- Incorporate authentic materials and real-world contexts that mirror actual language use situations.
- Provide clear and concise instructions for each test section.
- Ensure that the test items are free from cultural, gender, or other biases.

Practicality

Practicality is a critical aspect of language assessment, focusing on the feasibility, efficiency, and resource requirements of implementing a test. It encompasses considerations such as the time, cost, and technical requirements needed to design, administer, and score the test, as well as the ease with which educators can interpret and use the results. Practicality ensures that assessments are not only theoretically sound and reliable but also accessible and manageable for instructors and institutions.

Essential Aspects of Practicality in Language Assessment

- **Test Administration**: Practicality involves the ease and feasibility of administering a test within the available logistical constraints, including time limits and physical space requirements. It also considers the need for specialized equipment or software (Bachman & Palmer, 2010).
- **Scoring and Interpretation**: The process for scoring a test should be straightforward, reliable, and not overly time-consuming. Moreover, the results should be easy to interpret and applicable to the intended educational or evaluative purposes (Alderson, Clapham, & Wall, 1995).

- **Cost-effectiveness**: Assessments should offer a balance between the benefits they provide and the costs associated with their development, administration, and scoring. This includes direct financial costs as well as indirect costs, such as the time teachers spend preparing students for the test (Coombe, Folse, & Hubley, 2007).
- **Accessibility and Equity**: The practicality of an assessment also entails its accessibility to all students, including those with special needs, and its fairness in evaluating students from diverse backgrounds and with varying levels of proficiency (Kunnan, 2004).
- **Impact on Teaching and Learning**: Practical assessments should align with instructional goals and curricula, supporting teaching and learning processes rather than detracting from them. They should not require an excessive focus on test preparation at the expense of broader educational objectives (Shohamy, 2001).

Authenticity

Authenticity is a critical aspect of language assessment, as it helps ensure that the assessment accurately measures the language abilities of the test-taker. The authenticity of a language assessment refers to the degree to which the tasks and activities in the assessment resemble real-life language use. By having an authentic language assessment, the results can provide a more accurate and reliable representation of the test-taker's language abilities. It can also help to reduce the potential for test-takers to use rote memorization or other strategies that may not reflect their true language abilities.

Moreover, authentic language assessments can provide a more meaningful and relevant learning experience for test-takers. By engaging with tasks and activities that are similar to those they may encounter in real life, they can develop and refine their language skills in a more practical and relevant context. In summary, the authenticity of a language assessment is important as it helps to ensure that the results accurately reflect the test-taker's language abilities and provide a meaningful and relevant learning experience.

Examples of authenticity in assessment

1. A listening task that simulates a phone conversation between friends discussing weekend plans, with background noise and natural interruptions, captures authentic language use.
2. A writing task that requires composing a formal business email rather than a casual text message demonstrates an understanding of contextual appropriateness.
3. A listening assessment that includes speakers with diverse accents (British, American, Australian) acknowledges the variations in English language usage.

Fairness Issues

Fairness in language assessment ensures that all test-takers have an equal opportunity to demonstrate their language skills, irrespective of their cultural, social, or economic backgrounds. Fir assessments strive to minimize biases based on cultural, socio-economic, or linguistic factors that could lead to differential outcomes. Fairness involves providing necessary accommodations, such as extended time or alternative formats, to ensure that test-takers with disabilities or special needs are not disadvantaged.

Examples of the violation of fairness in Language Assessment

1. A listening task that includes culturally specific references unfamiliar to some test-takers, inadvertently favoring those from the culture being referenced.
2. A writing assessment that penalizes non-native speakers for minor grammatical errors, disproportionately affecting their scores compared to native speakers.
3. A speaking test that marks down individuals with regional accents or dialects, despite their clear communication, due to the bias towards a particular accent.
4. An assessment that requires a stable internet connection and the use of specific software, disadvantaging students who do not have access to such technology.

The Relationship between Reliability and Validity

Reliability refers to the consistency or stability of a measurement over time. In other words, a reliable measurement should produce consistent results if repeated multiple times under the same conditions. For example, if a measuring tool is reliable, it should produce similar results when used to measure the same construct at different times or by different raters. Validity refers to the accuracy or truthfulness of a measurement. In other words, a valid measurement should accurately reflect the construct it is intended to measure. For example, if a measuring tool is valid, it should accurately measure what it is intended to measure and not be influenced by extraneous factors.

There are several ways to assess the relationship between reliability and validity. A test must be reliable in order to be valid. Validity is related to accuracy, while reliability is related to consistency. A valid test cannot be obtained from an unreliable one. It is possible for a test to be reliable without being valid, though. It is often necessary for a test to be both valid and reliable. As mentioned before, reliability is used to determine the consistency of tests and results. Validity is measured by the agreement between test results and what the test is intended to measure. You can measure your confidence by using the height of an individual, for instance. There may be several consistent results that make the test reliable, but that does not mean it is valid. It has nothing to do with a person's height when it comes to confidence. It is highly likely that the validity and reliability of a test are high, which indicates that the test is effective and efficient. A test is valid if it measures what it is supposed to measure. Therefore, multiple choice tests are generally not an appropriate means of testing speaking ability; neither is a gap-fill test an appropriate means of determining whether or not a student knows how to use a grammar structure in communication. The presentation of a student may, on the other hand, serve as a valid basis for assessing a student's speaking ability, and a test that elicits a target grammar structure would reveal a student's grammar abilities.

A reliable assessment would yield the same results for that student if administered by a different person or in a different location. Class presentations and role-plays assessed by teachers are unlikely to be reliable because the test conditions cannot be replicated in another class. Test reliability is certainly a hallmark of the TOEFL iBT, which features highly detailed protocols to ensure uniformity of the experience for all students and two-rater grading for writing and speaking tasks. Clearly, the more validity, the harder it is to attain reliability; the more reliability, the harder it is to make the test valid (in the three-hour iBT, no human interaction is required). Valid tests can be made more reliable by implementing the following measures.

- Use a common set of learning objectives across the program and hold teachers accountable for teaching them.
- Use standard assessment rubrics across the program.
- Calibrate grading through teacher training.
- Have more than one person assess each student's performance.

In order for a measurement to be considered trustworthy, it must be both reliable and valid. In summary, reliability refers to consistency over time, while validity refers to accuracy. Both are important for ensuring that measurements are trustworthy and can be used to make valid conclusions.

Correlation in Language Assessment

A major concept for understanding reliability in assessment revolves around correlation. Correlation serves as a tool for determining the extent of the connection between two variables. In the context of reliability, this connection is established between the administration of an assessment instrument and the dependent variable. The instrument's reliability increases as the strength of this connection intensifies.

Correlation stands as a statistical technique employed to quantify the association between two variables. These variables might comprise two instances of the same test being administered, the administration of comparable versions of the same test, the correlation between a specific test and academic achievement, or even the interplay between factors like study time and final exam scores. In essence, correlation aids in determining whether two variables share a connection and, if so, the magnitude of that association. Within the realm of variable connections, three correlation types emerge: positive, negative, and no discernible relationship. Expressing the degree of connection between two variables, a correlation coefficient (r) comes into play. Correlation typically ranges from -1 to 1. A value of 1 indicates a perfect positive correlation, while -1 indicates a perfect negative correlation. A value of 0 indicates no linear correlation. The correlation coefficient is a numerical measure that quantifies the strength and direction of a linear relationship between two continuous variables. There are different types of correlation coefficients, but one of the most commonly used is the Pearson correlation coefficient.

The close to 1.00 the coefficient (r), the stronger the degree of the relationship between the two variables. Hence, an r value of .82 indicates a more potent relationship compared to an r value of .61. It's worth noting that in correlation coefficients, the presence of a positive or negative sign doesn't indicate the intensity of the connection; rather, it signifies the direction of the relationship. Consequently, correlation values of .85 and -.85 indicate equal strength. The use of correlation in language assessment, though, is not without issues and limitations, and it is important to be aware of these when interpreting and using the results of correlation-based studies. Correlation coefficients can only indicate the presence of a relationship between two variables, not the cause-and-effect relationship.

This means that correlation-based predictions may not be accurate and may lead to incorrect decisions about language assessment and instruction. Correlation is a measure of linear relationship between two variables, but not all relationships are linear. This means that correlation may not accurately capture complex relationships between language ability and other factors. Additionally, it does not indicate causation; thus, the correlation between two variables does not necessarily signify that changes in one variable cause changes in the other.

Positive Correlation

A positive correlation signifies a connection between variables that move in the same direction. In simpler terms, when the scores of one variable within a dataset rise, the corresponding scores of the other variable also exhibit an upward trend. Conversely, when one variable's scores decrease, the scores of the other variable follow decrease. To illustrate, consider the following array of scores. Students who achieved high scores on a reading ability test also displayed high grammar test scores. Consequently, the data suggests a positive correlation between the reading test scores (variable X) and the student's grammar test scores (variable Y).

Negative Correlation

In the realm of negative correlation, a scenario unfolds where high scores on one variable correspond with low scores on another variable. Instances of likely negative correlations include the number of days absent and final grades, and the number of work hours missed and the amount of hourly payment. When the bond between variables is weak, the scatterplot lacks a well-defined line. A scatterplot's diminished linearity directly reflects a weaker correlation.

Figure 3.3

Examples of positive correlation and negative correlation

positive correlation

students	reading test	grammar test
1	33	20
2	35	31
3	41	37
4	50	50
5	55	52
6	63	61
7	72	70
8	85	82

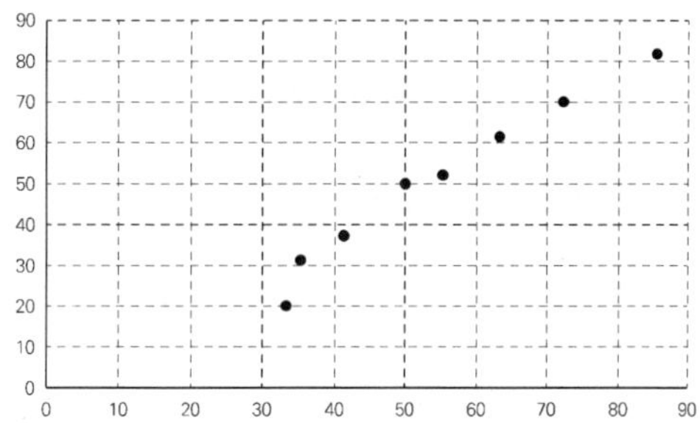

negative correlation

students	reading test	math test
1	22	82
2	35	73
3	41	65
4	50	54
5	62	48
6	68	42
7	72	35
8	81	28

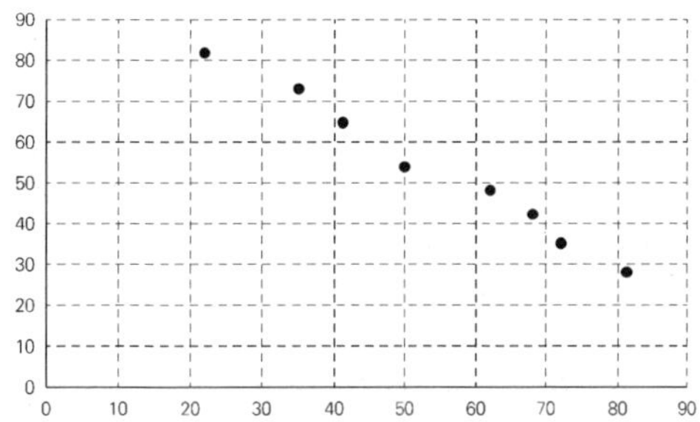

EXERCISES

Match the following terms with the correct definitions. Terms may be used more than once.

1. reliability	6. concurrent validity
2. content-related validity	7. washback effect
3. variability	8. correlation
4. construct-related Validity	9. bias
5. validity	10. predictive validity

1. __________ refers to the consistency and stability of assessment results, indicating the degree to which a test yields consistent scores when administered under similar conditions.

2. __________ refers to the degree to which a test measures the specific construct or trait it intends to assess, providing evidence that the test is measuring what it claims to measure.

3. __________ assesses whether the content of the test is relevant, representative, and sufficiently comprehensive to measure the targeted construct or skill.

4. Establishing __________ involves gathering evidence to support that the test measures what it is intended to measure and that the interpretations and inferences drawn from the test scores are appropriate.

5. A reliable test produces consistent results, with little __________ in scores when the same students take the test on different occasions.

6. __________ is a type of validity that examines the relationship between the scores of a test and the scores of a comparable test or measure administered at the same time.

7. ___________ refers to the impact of an assessment on teaching and learning, influencing how teachers teach and students learn based on the format and content of the test.

8. ___________ is a statistical measure that assesses the strength and direction of the relationship between two variables, such as test scores and performance.

9. To promote fairness, it's essential to minimize potential sources of ___________ that could advantage or disadvantage specific groups of students.

10. ___________ is a type of criterion-related validity that examines how well a test predicts future performance on a related criterion.

PART II

Developing Assessment Tools in the classroom

UNIT 4.

Test Specification

Key Points

In this unit you will be able to:

1. Understand the concept of test specification in language testing
2. Create test specifications for a specific test
3. Develop effective test items for a specific test

The introduction of the Test Specification

This unit outlines the key components and steps involved in the development of language assessments. It emphasizes the importance of creating detailed test specifications to guide the test development process, ensuring that assessments are valid, reliable, and fair. The unit aims to equip learners with the ability to understand test specification concepts, create specific test specifications for a given test, and develop effective test items. This introduction sets the stage for a deeper exploration into the systematic approach to language testing, including defining the purpose and context of a test, identifying the content domain, determining the test format, and considering accessibility and accommodations, among other steps.

What is Test Specification in L2 Testing?

Test specification is a fundamental component in the development of language assessments, detailing the objectives, content, format, and evaluation criteria of a language test. It acts as a comprehensive blueprint, guiding the test creation process to ensure the assessment's validity, reliability, and fairness. Test specifications describe the achievement domain, specifying the language skills, content areas, and cognitive levels to be assessed, thereby providing a clear direction for test development. Firstly, test specifications vividly describe the achievement domain that the test aims to measure. This involves clearly outlining the specific language skills, content areas, and cognitive levels that the test will assess. By detailing the scope of the assessment, test specifications provide a clear roadmap for test developers, ensuring that the test content accurately reflects the intended language proficiency.

Secondly, test specifications offer valuable guidelines for obtaining a representative sample of test tasks. They outline the distribution of task types, content coverage, and difficulty levels to be included in the assessment. This systematic approach ensures that the test adequately assesses a diverse range of language skills and challenges, preventing an overemphasis on certain skills or content areas. As a result, the test becomes a comprehensive tool that captures learners' multifaceted language abilities, supporting fair and balanced evaluation. In essence, test specifications serve as a foundational framework that shapes every aspect of the assessment process. By delineating the achievement domain and providing task distribution guidelines, they ensure that the resulting test is valid, reliable, and reflective of the desired language proficiency standards. The following are some of the key steps of test specification in language testing:

Figure 4.1

Steps of Test Specification in L2 language Testing

Step 1	**Define the Purpose and Context of the Test** Identify the purpose of the test Determine the target audience Consider the testing context (e.g., classroom-based or high-stakes).
Step 2	**Identify the Content Domain** Determine the specific language skills and subskills to be assessed (e.g., reading, listening, speaking, writing). Identify the content areas or themes relevant to the test (e.g., travel, daily life, academic topics).
Step 3	**Determine the Test Format** Choose appropriate item types (e.g., multiple-choice, short response, fill-in-the-blanks) based on the skills being assessed. Decide on the structure of the test (e.g., sections, no of items per section). Consider the balance of item difficulty and item discrimination.
Step 4	**Develop Test Specifications** Define the content coverage for each skill Specify the cognitive levels required for different tasks (e.g., comprehension, analysis, synthesis). Set the time limits for each section or task.
Step 5	**Consider Accessibility and Accommodations** Ensure that the test is accessible to diverse learners, including those with special needs. Plan for accommodations (e.g., extended time, larger font size, audio options) based on the test-takers' requirements.

Step 6	**Pilot Testing and Revision** Develop a small-scale version of the test and administer it to a representative sample of learners. Analyze the results to identify potential issues with item clarity, difficulty, or bias. Revise and refine the test items and specifications based on pilot test outcomes.
Step 7	**Review and Validation** Share the test specifications with language experts, educators, and stakeholders for feedback. Ensure that the specifications align with established language proficiency standards or frameworks.
Step 8	**Finalization and Production** Incorporate the feedback and finalize the test specifications. Develop the complete test, including items, instructions, and scoring guidelines. Prepare any necessary administration materials.
Step 9	**Implementation and Analysis** Administer the test to the intended audience under controlled conditions. Collect test responses and data from test-takers. Analyze the test results to assess the quality of the assessment, including reliability and validity.

In conclusion, test specification is an important aspect of language testing that involves defining the objectives, content, format, and criteria for evaluating the results of a language test. The quality and effectiveness of a language test will depend on the care and attention given to the test specification process. Each step in the process contributes to the creation of a well-structured and effective language assessment that aligns with its intended purpose and accurately measures learners' language abilities.

Writing Up Test Specification

Creating a comprehensive test specification is a crucial step in the assessment development process. A well-written test specification outlines the purpose, content, format, and administration of the assessment. Here's examples of test specifications with specific test purposes:

Scenario for a Reading Quiz

In a secondary school English class, the teacher is preparing a reading quiz to assess the students' comprehension skills. The quiz is based on a short passage about an upcoming school event. The purpose of the quiz is to gauge students' ability to understand main ideas, details, and make inferences from the text. The quiz will consist of multiple-choice questions, true/false statements, and a short written response. The teacher aims to create a balanced assessment that aligns with the curriculum and encourages students to engage with the reading material.

Test Specification Steps

1. Define the purpose and context

The purpose of this quiz is to assess secondary school students' reading comprehension skills by evaluating their understanding of a passage related to an upcoming school event. The quiz aims to determine students' ability to identify main ideas, extract details, and draw inferences from the text.

2. Identify the content domain

The passage selected for the quiz centers around a school event announcement. The content domain includes comprehension of main ideas, event details, and implied information. The quiz will not assess vocabulary in isolation but will focus on holistic understanding of the text.

3. Determine the test format

The quiz will comprise a combination of multiple-choice questions, true/false statements, and one short written response. The multiple-choice questions will assess main ideas and specific details, while the true/false statements will require students to identify accurate information from the text. The short written response will prompt students to reflect on the implications of the event and provide a brief explanation.

4. Develop test specifications

- Multiple-choice questions: Develop five questions that cover main ideas, details, and inference-based questions. Each question should have four options.
- True/false statements: Create three statements that are directly related to the passage. Ensure that one true statement and one false statement are well-balanced to avoid predictability.
- Short written response: Design a prompt that asks students to explain the significance of the event and its potential impact on the school community in 3-5 sentences.

5. Consider accessibility and accommodations

Provide clear and concise instructions for each question. Ensure that the font size and layout are visually accessible for all students. If needed, offer additional time for students with special needs to complete the quiz.

Scenario for L2 Writing Final Exam

As the school year comes to an end, secondary school students are preparing for their L2 writing final exam. The exam is designed to evaluate their proficiency in expressing ideas coherently and effectively through written communication. The purpose of the exam is to assess their ability to construct well-structured paragraphs, utilize appropriate vocabulary and grammar, and convey their thoughts clearly. The exam consists of two parts: a short essay and a creative writing piece. The goal is to provide a comprehensive assessment that aligns with the curriculum and encourages students to showcase their writing skills.

Test Specification Steps

1. Define the purpose and context

The purpose of the L2 writing final exam is to evaluate secondary school students' writing abilities by assessing their capacity to construct organized and coherent pieces of writing. The exam aims to measure their proficiency in using appropriate vocabulary, grammar, and sentence structures to convey ideas effectively.

2. Identify the content domain

The exam will cover two main types of writing: expository and creative. The content domain includes crafting well-structured paragraphs, utilizing varied vocabulary, demonstrating grammatical accuracy, and showcasing creativity in narrative writing.

3. Determine the test format

The exam will consist of two parts. Part one will require students to write a short essay in response to a given prompt. Part two will involve a creative writing task, where students can choose to write a short story, poem, or descriptive piece.

4. Develop test specifications

- Short Essay (Part One): Provide a prompt that presents a specific topic or issue for students to discuss. For example, "Write a short essay explaining the importance of environmental conservation and suggesting ways individuals can contribute."
- Creative Writing (Part Two): Offer students multiple options, such as writing a short story about a mysterious adventure or crafting a descriptive paragraph about their favorite place.

5. Consider accessibility and accommodations

Ensure that the prompts are clear and concise. Consider providing a word bank or vocabulary suggestions to support students who may struggle with vocabulary selection. Offer extra time for students with special needs to complete the exam if necessary.

6. Review and validation

Share the exam with fellow language educators or experts to ensure that the prompts accurately assess the targeted writing skills and align with the curriculum objectives.

7. Finalization and production

Incorporate any revisions based on feedback and finalize the exam. Organize the prompts in a logical order, ensuring that they cater to the two distinct writing types.

8. Implementation and analysis

Administer the exam to the secondary school students. Evaluate their responses to assess their ability to construct coherent essays and showcase creativity in their creative writing pieces.

A holistic scoring rubric can be used to evaluate the L2 writing final exam with different levels of performance. Each level is accompanied by a description of what the student's writing would typically demonstrate at that level. This holistic scoring rubric provides a comprehensive framework for assessing student performance on the L2 writing final exam. It considers various aspects of writing, including organization, vocabulary, language usage, grammar, mechanics, and creative elements, providing clear descriptors for each level of performance.

Score	Description
5 Excellent (A)	The writing is exceptionally clear, well-organized, and engaging. The student effectively conveys ideas using a wide range of vocabulary and precise language. Grammar and mechanics are virtually error-free, enhancing the overall coherence of the composition. Creative elements in the narrative showcase originality and depth.
4 Proficient (B)	The writing is clear and organized, with a good flow of ideas. The student demonstrates proficiency in vocabulary and language usage, with minor errors. Grammar and mechanics are generally sound, contributing to coherence. Creative elements in the narrative display creativity and imagination.
3 Adequate (C)	The writing is mostly clear and organized, though some areas may lack smooth transitions. The student uses a satisfactory range of vocabulary and language, with occasional errors that do not hinder comprehension. Grammar and mechanics are generally correct, but some errors may affect clarity. Creative elements in the narrative show basic creativity.

Score	Description
2 Limited (D)	The writing may lack organization and coherence, making it challenging to follow. Vocabulary and language use are limited, leading to repetitive or awkward phrasing. Grammar and mechanics errors are noticeable and may hinder understanding. Creative elements in the narrative are minimal.
1 Insufficient (F)	The writing lacks organization, coherence, and clarity. Vocabulary and language use are inadequate, leading to significant difficulty in understanding. Grammar and mechanics errors are frequent and impede comprehension. Creative elements in the narrative are absent or ineffective.

Illustrative Action Verbs for Defining Objectives

The examples of action verbs for defining objectives serve a pivotal role in the development of test specifications, enhancing the precision and effectiveness of the assessment process. Illustrative action verbs provide clear and explicit descriptions of the cognitive actions associated with each learning objective. When incorporated into test specifications, they ensure that the assessment tasks are aligned with the specific skills and knowledge intended to be assessed. This alignment enhances the clarity of the test specifications, guiding test developers in creating assessment items that accurately reflect the targeted learning outcomes.

Table 4.1

Illustrative Action Verbs for Defining Objectives in the Cognitive Domain of the Revised Bloom's Taxonomy (Gronlund, 2006)

Taxonomy Categories	Sample Verbs for Stating Specific Learning Outcomes
Remember	Identifies, names, defines, describes, lists, matches, selects outlines
Understand	Classifies, explains, summarizes, converts, predicts, interprets, illustrates
Apply	Demonstrates, computes, solves, modifies, arranges, operates, relates, uses
Analyze	Differentiates, diagrams, estimates, separates, orders, subdivides, distinguishes between
Evaluate	Judges, criticizes, compares, justifies, concludes, discriminates, detects
Create	Combines, creates, formulates, designs, composes, constructs, rearranges, revises.

Types of Test Items: Multiple-choice, Cloze test, Short-response, Essay

Those are all types of test items that are commonly used in L2 language assessment including multiple-choice, cloze, short response, essay items. These are just a few examples of the different types of test items that can be used to assess a range of skills and knowledge. The type of test item used will depend on the objectives of the assessment and the skills being assessed. In the following section, we'll discuss how to develop an effective multiple-choice and cloze test item.

Developing Multiple-choice Items

Developing multiple-choice items for an L2 language test involves careful alignment with the test specifications to ensure that the items effectively measure the intended language skills and learning outcomes. Here's a step-by-step guide on how to develop multiple-choice items.

Figure 4.2

Stages of Multiple-choice Items Development

Step 1: Create Clear Item Stems Write clear and concise item stems that present a question or a statement related to the learning objectives. Ensure that the stem is grammatically correct and free from ambiguity.

Step 2: Develop Plausible Distractors For each multiple-choice item, create a set of answer choices that include one correct answer (the "key") and several plausible distractors. The distractors should be realistic and related to common student misconceptions. This step requires careful consideration to ensure that the distractors are appropriate and avoid any misleading or confusing options.

Step 3: Maintain Consistent Language Ensure that the language used in the item stems and answer choices is consistent with the language proficiency level of the students. Avoid using complex sentence structures or advanced vocabulary that might confuse test takers.

Step 4: Balance Distractor Difficulty The distractors should be evenly distributed in terms of difficulty. Avoid having all the distractors too easy or too difficult. The correct answer should not always be the longest or the shortest option.

Step 5: Reflect Bloom's Taxonomy Levels Align the multiple-choice items with the cognitive levels specified in the test specifications. This could range from recalling facts to analyzing information. The items should reflect a range of cognitive skills.

Step 6: Consider Context If the items are related to reading comprehension or listening, ensure that the context is meaningful and supports the understanding of the question. The context should not be too lengthy or distracting.

Step 7: Review and Validation Share the items with colleagues or language experts to ensure that they accurately assess the targeted language skills and align with the test specifications.

Developing Cloze Tests

Developing a cloze test for an L2 language test involves a systematic process that aligns with the test specifications. Here are the steps to create an effective cloze test after considering all the necessary content domain and testing context.

Step 1. Develop the Passage: Create a passage that is suitable for the proficiency level of the students and aligns with the content domain. The passage should be engaging, coherent, and convey meaningful context.

Example

Original Passage: Last summer, I had the opportunity to visit a __(1)__ island in the Pacific Ocean. The island was known for its breathtaking __(2)__ and clear blue waters. I spent my days exploring the lush forests and __(3)__ sandy beaches.

Step 2. Determine the Deletion Strategy: Decide which words or phrases will be deleted from the passage. Consider which words are crucial for comprehension and which ones can be omitted to create gaps for students to fill.

Example

Deletion Strategy: Delete words related to descriptive details and essential nouns.

Step 3. Develop Test Specifications: Based on the content domain, create specific gaps that align with the intended language skills. The gaps should challenge students to use their vocabulary and contextual understanding to fill in the missing words.

Example

Content Domain: Travel

Gaps:				
1)	A) remote	B) crowded	C) bustling	D) vast
2)	A) landscapes	B) cities	C) mountains	D) oceans
3)	A) rocky	B) polluted	C) pristine	D) deserted

Step 4. Pilot Testing and Revision: Administer the cloze test to a small group of students to identify any confusing or ambiguous gaps. Use their feedback to revise and refine the context and wording of the gaps.

Step 5. Review and Validation: Share the cloze test with fellow educators or experts to ensure that it accurately assesses the targeted language skills and aligns with the curriculum objectives.

Elicitation/Response Mode in Test Construction

Elicitation (oral/written) Mode

Elicitation mode refers to the method used to prompt or extract responses from the test takers. It determines how the test content is presented to the students and how they are expected to provide their answers. Elicitation modes can be broadly categorized into two main categories: oral and written. In the oral mode, learners are required to respond using spoken language. This could involve answering questions, engaging in conversations, participating in interviews, or delivering oral presentations. Oral elicitation is particularly useful for assessing speaking and listening skills. For example, in a language test, learners might be asked to respond to questions or describe a given picture orally. In the written mode, learners are expected to respond in written form. This can include tasks such as completing sentences, writing essays, solving mathematical problems, and answering multiple-choice questions. Written elicitation is commonly used to assess reading and writing skills. For instance, in a language test, students might be required to write an essay or complete a fill-in-the-blank exercise.

Response (oral/written) Mode

Response mode refers to how learners provide their answers or demonstrate their understanding in response to the prompts or tasks presented in the test. Just like elicitation modes, response modes can also be categorized into oral and written forms. In the oral response mode, students provide their answers using spoken language. This could involve giving verbal explanations, responses, or presentations. Oral responses are often used to assess speaking and listening skills. For instance, students might be asked to explain a concept, participate in a role-play, or respond to interview questions orally.

In the written response mode, students provide their answers in written form. This could include writing short paragraphs, essays, or solving problems using written language. Written responses are commonly used to assess reading and writing skills. For example, students might be required to write an essay on a given topic or complete a written comprehension exercise. The choice of elicitation and response modes in test construction depends on the specific skills being assessed, the learning objectives, and the nature of the content being tested. Both modes offer unique advantages and challenges, and careful consideration is necessary to ensure that the chosen modes effectively measure the desired abilities and accurately reflect the students' proficiency.

Figure 4.3

Elicitation and Response Modes in Test Construction
(adopted from Brown & Abeywickrama (2019, p. 67))

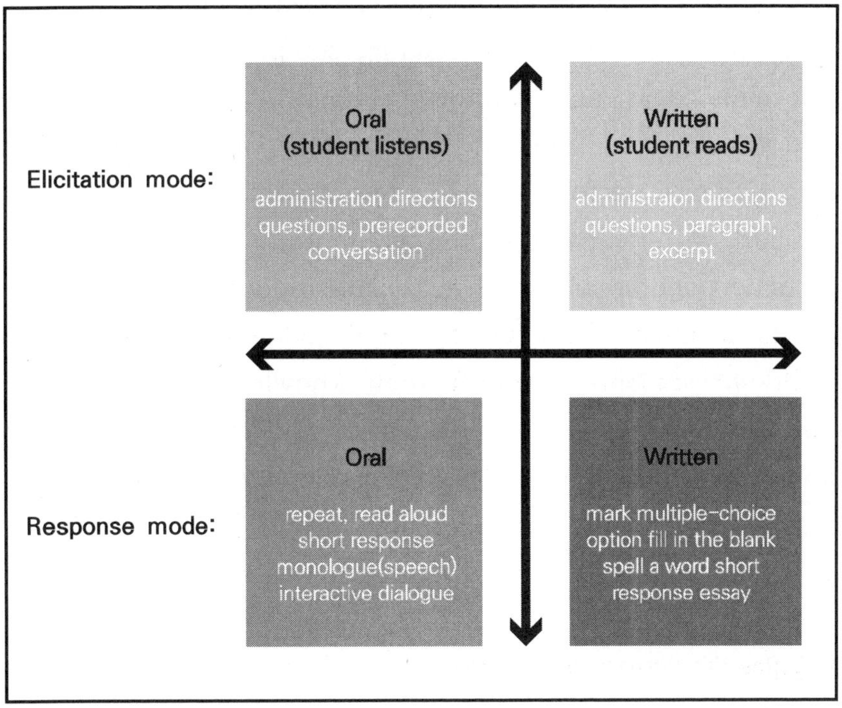

Test Development Example: English Reading Achievement Test

Statement of the Problem

The English reading achievement test aims to address the following question: How effectively do high school students comprehend and analyze literary texts after completing a specific unit on literature? This test seeks to evaluate students' reading comprehension skills, ability to identify main ideas and supporting details, inferencing capabilities, vocabulary usage in context, and critical analysis techniques. By assessing students' performance in these areas, the test aims to provide insights into the effectiveness of the literature unit in enhancing their literary understanding and analytical skills. Additionally, the test aims to explore the alignment between the taught content, the test content, and the ability of students to apply their knowledge in interpreting and analyzing literary texts. The results of this test will contribute to informing instructional strategies and curriculum refinement in order to better prepare students for proficient reading and interpretation of literary works.

Step 1: Define the Purpose and Context

The purpose of this English Reading Achievement Test is to assess the reading comprehension skills of high school students. The test is intended to be administered at the end of a specific unit on literature. The context is a classroom setting, and the test aims to measure students' ability to understand and analyze literary texts.

Step 2: Identify the Content Domain

The content domain includes various types of literary texts, such as short stories and poems. The test will cover aspects like main ideas, supporting details, inferencing, vocabulary in context, and literary analysis techniques.

Step 3: Determine the Test Format

The test will consist of two sections: Multiple-Choice Questions (MCQs) and Short-Answer Questions (SAQs). The MCQs will assess comprehension skills, while the SAQs will focus on critical analysis and interpretation of the texts.

Step 4: Develop Test Specifications

- The test will have 20 MCQs, evenly distributed among the different content areas.
- Each MCQ will have four answer options, with only one correct answer.
- The SAQ section will have 5 questions, requiring students to provide detailed responses and explanations.

Step 5: Consider Accessibility and Accommodations

Accommodations will be provided for students with special needs, such as extended time and enlarged font size.

Step 6: Pilot Testing and Revision

A pilot test will be administered to a small group of students to identify any unclear questions or issues with the test administration. Based on the pilot results, necessary revisions will be made.

Step 7: Review and Validation

The test specifications and questions will be reviewed by English language educators to ensure alignment with curriculum objectives and appropriate levels of difficulty.

Step 8: Finalization and Production

Final adjustments will be made based on feedback and validation results. The test will then be formatted and produced for administration.

Step 9: Implementation and Analysis

The test will be administered to the target student population. Responses will be collected and analyzed for reliability and validity. Statistical analysis will help determine item difficulty and discrimination.

By following these essential steps of test specification, the English Reading Achievement Test is developed with a clear purpose, appropriate content coverage, varied question formats, and accommodations for diverse learners. The resulting assessment effectively evaluates L2 learners' reading comprehension and literary analysis skills within the specified educational context.

EXERCISES

Match the following terms with the correct definitions. Terms may be used more than once.

1. item types	6. test specification
2. purpose	7. multiple-choice
3. elicitation	8. content
4. scoring rubrics	9. validity
5. test administration	10. response

1. A ___________ is a detailed plan that outlines the content, format, and administration of an assessment, ensuring that the test aligns with the intended purpose and accurately measures the desired language skills or knowledge.

2. The test specification should specify the ___________ that will be used in the assessment, such as multiple-choice, essay, speaking tasks, or listening exercises.

3. The first step in test specification development is to define the ___________ and intended outcomes of the assessment.

4. For a speaking test, the ___________ mode could involve the instruction to describe a picture or discussing a topic.

5. In a ___________ question item, test takers select the correct answer from a set of options.

6. ___________ for each item type should be provided in the test specification, outlining the criteria and guidelines for scoring and assigning points to different responses.

7. Details regarding the __________ of the assessment, including test location, timing, instructions, and procedures, should be outlined in the test specification.

8. After defining the purpose, the next step involves identifying the specific __________ or skills that the test will measure.

9. In test specification development, considering the __________ and fairness of the assessment is essential to ensure equal opportunities for all test takers.

UNIT 5.

Descriptive Statistics

Key Points

In this unit you will be able to:

1. Learn about the basic concepts of descriptive statistics: central tendency (mean, median, mode) and dispersion (range, variance, standard variation)
2. Understand the types of numerical scales and normal distribution
3. Know how to calculate standardized scores: t-score, z-score, percentile score, and percentile rank

Introduction to Descriptive Statistics in Test Analysis

Descriptive statistics play an essential role in analyzing and interpreting test results, offering a clear view of student performance to both test developers and stakeholders. This unit begins by exploring different scales for organizing numerical information and proceeds to introduce methods for visually representing data, emphasizing the frequency of score occurrences. Additionally, descriptive statistics provide another useful set of tools for describing sets of data, which covers statistics for describing the central tendency of a set of numbers, as well as for characterizing the dispersion of numbers away from the central tendency.

Core Concepts in Descriptive Statistics:

- **Types of Numerical Scales**: Understanding the distinctions between nominal, ordinal, interval, and ratio scales is foundational for accurately classifying and quantifying data in educational assessments.
- **Visual Data Display**: Techniques such as histograms, bar charts, and pie charts facilitate the intuitive presentation of score distributions and frequencies.
- **Central Tendency and Dispersion**: Key statistics, including the mean, median, mode (for central tendency), and range, variance, and standard deviation (for dispersion), provide insights into the overall performance patterns and variability among test scores.

Types of Numerical Scales

Numerical scales are used in various fields of research and data analysis to classify and quantify different types of data. There are four main types of numerical scales: nominal, ordinal, interval, and ratio scales. Each scale has its unique properties and level of measurement. First, the nominal scale is the lowest level of measurement and is used to categorize data into distinct groups or categories. The data is qualitative and cannot be ranked or quantified in a meaningful way. Nominal data is often represented by labels or names. Blood types (A, B, AB, O) are a classic example of nominal data. Other examples include gender (male, female), colors (red, blue, green), and vehicle types (car, truck, motorcycle).

The ordinal scale allows data to be ranked or ordered based on specific criteria, but the differences between categories are not standardized or precisely measurable. It provides information about the relative position or rank of data points. Education levels (elementary, high school, bachelor's degree, master's degree, Ph.D.) can be represented using an ordinal scale. Other examples include movie ratings (1 star, 2 stars, 3 stars, 4 stars, 5 stars) and customer satisfaction ratings (very dissatisfied, dissatisfied, neutral, satisfied, very satisfied).

The interval scale has all the properties of the ordinal scale and, in addition, allows for the measurement of the distance or interval between data points. However, it lacks a true zero point, meaning that zero does not indicate the absence of the measured attribute. Celsius temperature scales are examples of interval scales. A temperature of 20°C is not twice as hot as 10°C, but the difference between the two points (10°C) is the same as the difference between 30°C and 20°C.

Last, the ratio scale is the highest level of measurement and possesses all the properties of the previous scales. It allows for the ranking, precise measurement of intervals, and has a true zero point, indicating the absence of the measured attribute. Height, measured in centimeters or inches, exemplifies ratio measurement, where the zero point signifies the absence of height. Ratios between different heights can be formed, allowing for meaningful comparisons, such as assessing the height difference between two individuals. In summary, each numerical scale serves a specific purpose in data analysis, and researchers must carefully choose the appropriate scale depending on the nature of their data and the type of analysis they wish to conduct.

Table 5.1

Levels of Measurement

	Nominal	Ordinal	Interval	Ratio
Example	Blood type	Levels of satisfaction	Celcious temperature	Height
Category(Name)	✓	✓	✓	✓
Ranking order		✓	✓	✓
Equal Interval			✓	✓
True Zero Point				✓

Descriptive Statistics

Descriptive statistics serve as numerical representations showcasing the performance of a group of students on a test. As a vital branch of statistics, it focuses on organizing, summarizing, and interpreting data in a clear and concise manner. Its primary purpose is to describe and present the essential features of a dataset, providing a clear and concise overview of the information contained within it. Descriptive statistics do not involve making inferences or drawing conclusions beyond the data itself; instead, they focus on the characteristics of the data. There are two main types of descriptive statistics, which include central tendency (mean, median, mode) and dispersion (range, variance, standard variation).

Central Tendency

Central tendency refers to the measure or concept that represents the center or typical value of a dataset. It provides a way to summarize and describe the distribution of data by identifying a single value around which the data tend to cluster. There are three commonly used measures of central tendency: mean, median, and mode.

- **Mean**: The mean, also known as the average, is calculated by summing up all the values in a dataset and dividing by the total number of observations. It is sensitive to extreme values and can be affected by outliers. The mean is commonly used when the data follows a normal distribution.

$$\text{Mean} = \frac{\Sigma X}{N}$$

M = mean
N = number of scores
X = scores
Σ = sum of all scores

- **Median**: The median is the middle value of a dataset when it is arranged in ascending or descending order. If there is an even number of observations, the median is calculated as the average of the two middle values. The median is less sensitive to extreme values and outliers, making it useful for skewed or non-normal distributions. In the set of 100, 90, 72, 64, 55, 47, 30, the median is 64, as it represents the middle value of the dataset in ascending order.

- **Mode**: The mode represents the most frequently occurring value(s) in a dataset. Unlike the mean and median, the mode is not a measure of central tendency in the strictest sense, as it does not consider the entire dataset. The mode is particularly useful for categorical or discrete data, where it identifies the most common category or value.

Example

Central tendency of reading scores

Consider the following English reading scores of 10 students:
78, 85, 92, 65, 78, 88, 92, 70, 78, 81.

Mean: (78 + 85 + 92 + 65 + 78 + 88 + 92 + 70 + 78 + 81) / 10 = 80.7

Median: Arrange the data in ascending order:
65, 70, 78, 78, 78, 81, 85, 88, 92, 92.

The median is the average of the two middle values, i.e., (78 + 81) / 2 = 79.5.

Mode: The mode is 78 since it appears three times, more than any other value.

These measures provide different perspectives on the center of the data and are chosen based on the nature of the dataset and the research question. They help to summarize and simplify complex datasets, making them more interpretable and facilitating comparisons between different groups or conditions.

Dispersion

Measures of Dispersion provides information about the spread or dispersion of the data points in a dataset. The three common measures of dispersion are:

- **Range**: The difference between the largest and smallest values in the dataset. It gives a rough idea of the spread of the data. However, the range indicates the extent of variability between the highest and lowest scores, and it can be heavily influenced by any test performance that is not truly representative of the entire group of students. Such a student may be considered an outlier, who do not belong to the typical characteristics of the group.

- **Standard Deviation**: Standard deviation is a measure of how much the individual data points in a dataset deviate from the mean value. It quantifies the dispersion or spread of data points and provides valuable information about the variability within the dataset. A larger standard deviation indicates greater variability, while a smaller standard deviation suggests that data points are closer to the mean. The formula for the population standard deviation is:

$$\mathrm{SD} = \sqrt{\frac{\Sigma (X-M)^2}{N}}$$

M = mean
N = number of scores
X = scores
Σ = sum

- **Variance**: A measure of how much the data points deviate from the mean. It quantifies the average squared deviation of each data point from the mean.

Table 5.2

How to Calculate Standard Deviation

Student #	Score (X)	Mean (M)	$(X-M)^2$
1	85	71	$(85-71)^2 = 14^2 = 196$
2	90	71	$(90-71)^2 = 19^2 = 361$
3	70	71	$(70-71)^2 = (-1)^2 = 1$
4	65	71	$(65-71)^2 = (-6)^2 = 36$

Student #	Score (X)	Mean (M)	$(X-M)^2$
5	60	71	$(60-71)^2=(-11)^2=121$
6	90	71	$(90-71)^2=19^2=361$
7	75	71	$(75-71)^2=4^2=16$
8	65	71	$(65-71)^2=(-6)^2=36$
9	60	71	$(60-71)^2=(-11)^2=121$
10	50	71	$(50-71)^2=(-21)^2=441$
$\Sigma(X-M)^2 = 1{,}690$ $SD = \sqrt{\frac{\Sigma(X-M)^2}{N}} = \sqrt{\frac{1690}{10}} = 13$			

Example

Dispersion of English placement test scores

Consider the English placement test scores of 8 students in a class: 40, 50, 45, 55, 60, 70, 65, 80.

Range: Maximum value − Minimum value $= 80 - 40 = 40$

Standard Deviation:

Calculate the mean first: $(40+50+45+55+60+70+65+80)/8 = 58.125$

$$\frac{\Sigma(X-M)^2}{N} = [(40-58.125)^2 + (50-58.125)^2 + \cdots + (80-58.125)^2]/8 \approx 170.46$$

$$SD = \sqrt{170.46} \approx 13.05$$

Variance: 170.46

Exercise Items

1. Calculate the Mean Score: Given the test scores of five students in a English reading exam: 85, 72, 90, 78, and 88, calculate the mean score for this group of students.
2. Find the Mean, Median, and Mode: The reading comprehension scores of a group of ten students in English are as follows: 65, 72, 78, 82, 88, 90, 94, 96, 98, 100.
3. Identify the Mode: In an English vocabulary test, students were asked to list as many words as possible starting with the letter "A." The number of words listed by each student was: 12, 10, 8, 12, 14, 8, 12, 8. Identify the mode for the number of words listed.
4. Calculate the Range: In a grammar test, students' scores were as follows: 60, 72, 78, 85, 90, 92, 96. Determine the range of scores.
5. Compute the Standard Deviation: The speaking test scores of a group of English learners are: 85, 88, 90, 82, 95. Calculate the standard deviation of these scores.
6. Frequency Distribution: In an English pronunciation test, students were scored on a scale from 1(lowest) to 5(highest). The frequency of each scale was as follows: 1 points (2 students), 2 points (5 students), 3 points (10 students), 4 points (8 students), 5 points (15 students). Create a frequency distribution table for these grades.

point	Frequency

The Concept of Normal Distribution

A normal distribution is a specific type of probability distribution characterized by its bell-shaped curve. In this distribution, data clusters around the mean, with an equal number of data points on both sides, creating a symmetric pattern. The curve is defined by two parameters: the mean and the standard deviation. The mean represents the center of the distribution, and the standard deviation measures the spread or dispersion of the data points around the mean.

Figure 5.1

Normal Distribution of Scores

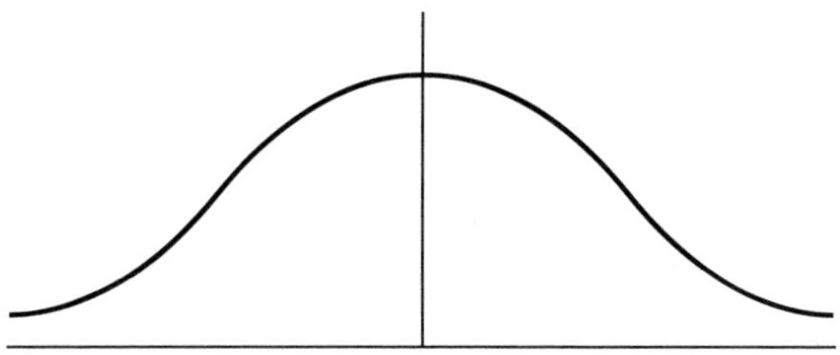

There are key characteristics of a normal distribution.

1. **Symmetry**: The curve is symmetrical, meaning that if it is folded along the vertical line passing through the mean, the two halves perfectly overlap.
2. **Bell-shaped curve**: The curve forms a smooth, bell-shaped pattern, with the highest point at the mean, and it tapers off as it moves away from the mean.
3. **Mean, median, and mode**: In a normal distribution, the mean, median, and mode are all equal and located at the center of the distribution.

4. **Empirical rule**: Approximately 68% of the data falls within one standard deviation of the mean, about 95% falls within two standard deviations, and nearly 99.7% falls within three standard deviations as shown in Figure 5.2.

Figure 5.2

Approximate Percentages under the Normal Distribution

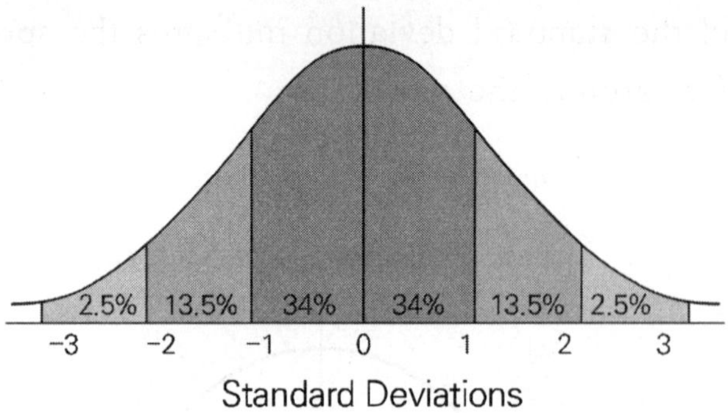

An example of a normal distribution is human height. If we were to measure the heights of a large group of adult individuals, we would typically observe a bell-shaped curve. Let's assume the mean height of this population is 170cm with a standard deviation of 6cm. The normal distribution of heights would look like this:

- Many individuals would have heights very close to the mean (170cm), creating the highest point on the curve.
- As we move away from the mean, there would be fewer individuals with heights that are significantly taller or shorter, resulting in the tapering edges of the bell-shaped curve.
- Approximately 68% of individuals would have heights within one standard deviation of the mean, which means heights between 164cm and 176cm (170cm ± 6cm).

- About 95% of individuals would have heights within two standard deviations of the mean, ranging from 158cm to 182cm (170cm ± (2 × 6cm)).
- Nearly 99.7% of individuals would have heights within three standard deviations of the mean, ranging from 152cm to 188cm (170cm ± (3 × 6cm)).

It's essential to understand normal distributions because they serve as a foundation for various statistical analyses, hypothesis testing, and modeling in numerous fields, including natural and social sciences, economics, and engineering.

Skewedness

In the context of language testing, a negatively skewed distribution and a positively skewed distribution refer to different patterns in the distribution of test scores. Skewness measures the asymmetry of a distribution, indicating whether the majority of scores are concentrated on one side of the distribution or the other. A negatively skewed distribution, also known as left-skewed, occurs when the tail of the distribution extends towards the lower end of the scale. In this type of distribution, the majority of test scores are concentrated towards the higher end, with fewer scores falling in the lower range.

Suppose a group of language learners takes a vocabulary test. If most of the learners perform well and score high marks on the test, but a few learners struggle and score significantly lower, it can result in a negatively skewed distribution. The majority of scores would be towards the higher end (high vocabulary proficiency), while a few scores would be on the lower end (lower vocabulary proficiency). On the other hand, a positively skewed distribution, also known as right-skewed, occurs when the tail of the distribution extends towards the higher end of the scale. In this type of distribution, the majority of test scores are concentrated towards the lower end, with fewer scores falling in the higher range. Consider a speaking proficiency test for a group of language learners. If most of the learners struggle with speaking fluency and score low marks, but a few learners excel and achieve high scores, it can result in a positively skewed distribution. The majority of scores would be towards the lower end (lower speaking proficiency), while a few scores would be on the higher end (higher speaking proficiency).

Skewedness in language testing can have implications for test design and interpretation of results. For instance, if a language test displays a positively skewed distribution, it could indicate that the test might not be effectively distinguishing between high-proficiency and low-proficiency students. It may also suggest that the test could be too challenging for most test-takers, potentially resulting in lower scores. On the other hand, a negatively skewed distribution might suggest that the test is generally more manageable for most test-takers. This could lead to some ceiling effects, as well as a potential lack of sufficiently challenging items. Understanding the distribution of scores helps test developers and educators identify areas of improvement in the test and adapt their teaching strategies accordingly.

Figure 5.3

Negatively Skewed, Normal, and Positively Skewed Distribution

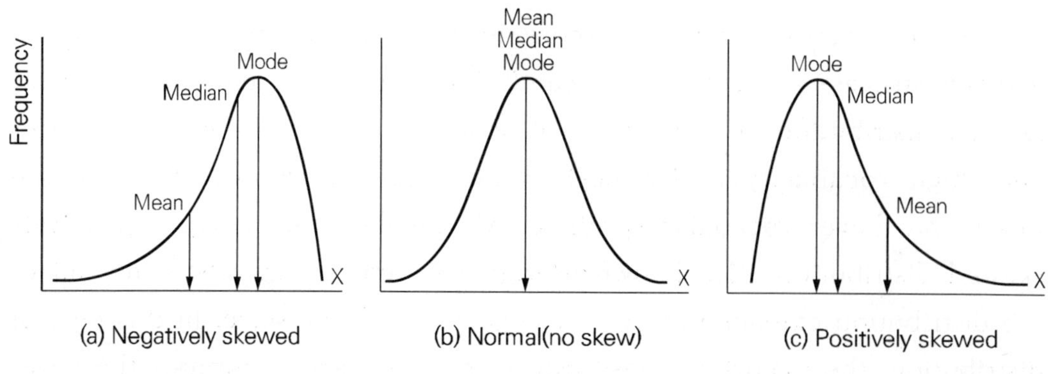

Application Exercises: Descriptive Statistics

Examine the descriptive statistics below and answer the questions that follow.

▌Summary of Test Statistics

Test	Number of Students (N)	Possible Scores	Mean (M)	SD
Grammar Test	100	50	35.2	6.45
Vocabulary Test	100	60	42.5	12.30
Reading Test	100	30	22.8	4.90
Total Proficiency Test	100	140	100.5	15.75
Spelling Test	100	20	16.0	3.50

1) Analyze the Grammar Test:

a. What is the mean score? ___________

b. What is the standard deviation? ___________

c. How many students took the test? ___________

2) Test Score Ranges:

a. Which test has the highest possible score? ___________

b. Which has the lowest? ___________

3) Participation Analysis:

a. Did any test have fewer participants than the others? ___________

b. Provide reasons for your answer. ___________

4) Score Dispersion:

a. Which test shows the greatest variability in scores? ___________

b. How can you tell? ___________

5) Additional Data:

What further details would be beneficial to fully understand these scores? ___________

Standardized Scores

Standardized scores are scores that have been transformed to have a standard mean and standard deviation. The process of standardizing scores allows for meaningful comparisons between different sets of data by removing the units of measurement and expressing each data point in terms of how many standard deviations it is above or below the mean. The commonly used types of standard scores include z-score, T-score, and percentiles.

- **Z-score**: The most common type of standardized score is the z-score, which is calculated using the formula. The z-score expresses how many standard deviations a particular data point is away from the mean. A positive z-score indicates that the data point is above the mean, while a negative z-score indicates that it is below the mean. A z-score of 0 means the data point is at the mean.

$$Z = \frac{X - M}{S}$$

X = Student's score
M = Mean
S = Standard Deviation

- **T-score**: T-scores are another type of standardized score, commonly used in educational and psychological testing. The T-score is defined as 50 + 10 × z-score. It shifts the z-scores to have a mean of 50 and a standard deviation of 10 as shown in Figure 5.4.

Figure 5.4

Presentation of z-score and T-score in the Normal Distribution

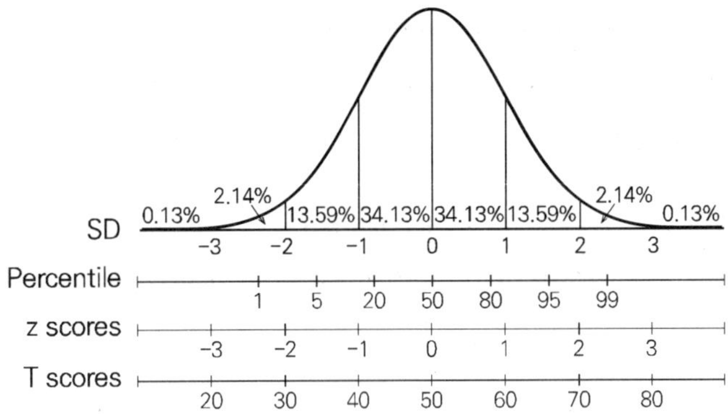

(adopted from Lange(2018))

- **Percentile score and percentile rank**: Percentile scores and ranks are not exactly z-scores, but they are often used for comparisons in a similar manner. They are calculated using cumulative distribution functions and are useful for understanding the relative standing of a data point within a distribution. Percentile scores and ranks are useful in understanding the distribution of a set of data, as they allow you to see where a particular score falls in relation to the rest of the data. They are commonly used in educational assessment, health sciences, and other areas where it is important to understand the distribution of data. A percentile score is a value that represents the percentage of a set of data that falls below a certain point. So percentile scores indicate how a given student's score relates to the test scores of the entire group of students. For example, if a student with a percentile score of 80 had a score equal to or higher than 80 percent of the other students in the distribution and a score equal to or lower than 20 percent.

You might know that you scored 67 out of 90 on a test. But that figure has no real meaning unless you know what percentile you fall into. If you know that your score is in the 85th percentile, that means you scored better than 85% of students who took the test. Percentiles are commonly used to report scores in tests, like the SAT, GRE and LSAT. for example, the 70th percentile on the 2013 GRE was 156. That means if you scored 156 on the exam, your score was better than 70 percent of test takers.

Figure 5.5

25th, 50th, 75th Percentile Scores

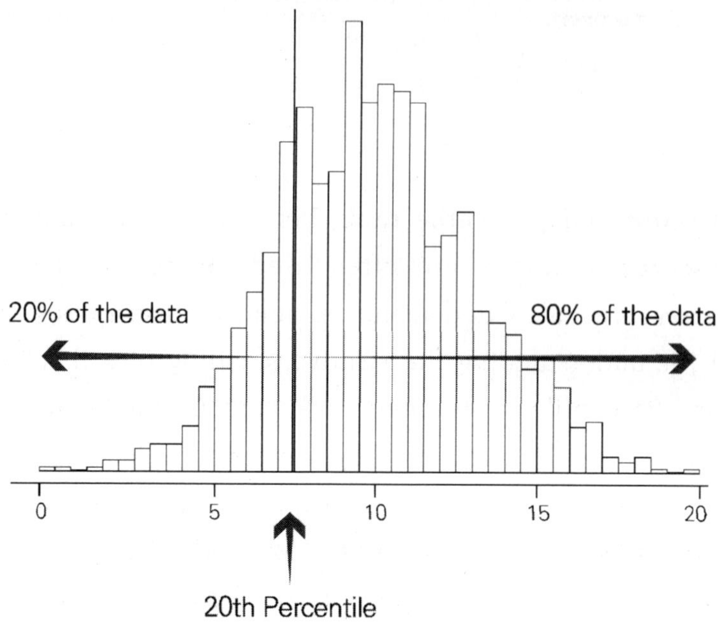

The 25th percentile is also called the first quartile.
The 50th percentile is generally the median
The 75th percentile is also called the third quartile.

So, in a nutshell, the percentile score is the value of the data, and the percentile rank is the rank of that value in the set of data. The formulas for calculating percentile score and percentile rank are as follows:

• **Percentile rank formula**: To calculate the percentiles, you first need to determine the rank of the individual's score among the entire group's scores.

$$\text{Percentile Rank(PR)} = \frac{\text{No. of scores below the score}}{\text{Total no. of scores}} \times 100$$

$$\text{Percentile Index} = \frac{\text{Percentile Rank(PR)}}{100} \times \text{Total no. of scores}$$

Example

1. Find the percentile rank for score 89.
[77, 76, 91, 90, 88, 85, 87, 78, 95, 90, 83, 89, 93, 75, 70, 67]

To find the percentile score using the provided formulas, we'll follow these steps:

1. Sort the scores in ascending order.
2. Calculate the percentile rank using the formula:
   (PR) = (No. of scores below the score / Total no. of scores) × 100
3. Calculate the percentile index using the formula:
   Percentile Index = (Percentile Rank / 100) × Total number of scores
4. Find the score corresponding to the percentile index.

Step 1: Count the number of scores below 89.
- Scores below 89: [77, 76, 88, 85, 87, 78, 83, 75, 70, 67]
- Number of scores below 89 = 10

Step 2: Calculate the percentile rank using the formula.
PR = (10 / 16) × 100 = 0.625 × 100 = 62.5^{th} percentile score

2. Find the score corresponding to 85th percentile score in the following test results.
[95, 88, 70, 75, 83, 70, 94, 66, 91, 68, 76, 82, 92, 91]

Step 1: Sort the scores in ascending order:
[66, 68, 70, 70, 75, 76, 82, 83, 88, 91, 91, 92, 94, 95]

Step 2: Cacluate Percentile Index = (85 / 100) × 14 = 11.9

Step 3: Identify the score corresponding to the 12th position in the sorted list. 85th percentile score = 92

Application Exercise: Percentile Rank

1. Find the percentile rank for a score of 90. __________
[85, 90, 75, 80, 85, 95, 70, 80, 90, 85, 80, 85, 90]

2. Find the score corresponding to the 75th percentile. __________
[72, 68, 80, 85, 90, 92, 75, 78, 82, 80, 88, 90, 70, 65]

3. Find the percentile rank for a score of 82. __________
[78, 85, 90, 92, 95, 68, 72, 75, 80, 82, 85, 88, 90, 70, 65]

4. Find the score corresponding to the 80th percentile. __________
[80, 75, 85, 92, 70, 78, 88, 95, 82, 80, 85, 90, 90, 68, 65, 70]

5. Find the percentile rank for a score of 75. __________
[85, 80, 90, 92, 95, 68, 70, 75, 78, 80, 82, 85, 88, 90, 90, 70, 65]

EXERCISES

Match the following terms with the correct definitions. Terms may be used more than once.

1. negatively skewed	7. central tendency
2. descriptive statistics	8. mode
3. positively skewed	9. numerical scales
4. range	10. mean
5. variance	11. median
6. standard deviation	12. normal distribution

1. ___________ is a measure that represents the central or typical value of a set of data points.

2. The ___________ is the value that occurs most frequently in a data set.

3. ___________ involves organizing, summarizing, and presenting data in a meaningful way to describe its main features and characteristics.

4. In a ___________ distribution, the tail extends toward the higher end of the scale, and the majority of data points are concentrated on the lower end.

5. The ___________ is the difference between the highest and lowest values in a data set, providing an indication of the data's spread.

6. ___________ are measurement scales that use numbers to represent quantities or levels of a variable, allowing for quantitative analysis and comparison.

7. The ___________ is calculated by summing all the data points and dividing the sum by the total number of data points.

8. __________ is a measure of how much the data points deviate from the mean, providing information about the data's dispersion.

9. In a __________ distribution, the tail extends toward the lower end of the scale, and the majority of data points are concentrated on the higher end.

10. __________ is the square root of the variance, and it represents the average amount by which data points deviate from the mean.

11. The __________ is the middle value in a data set when the data points are arranged in ascending or descending order.

12. In a __________, data clusters around the mean, creating a symmetric bell-shaped curve with equal data points on both sides.

UNIT 6.

Developing Scoring Criteria

Key Points

In this unit you will be able to:

1. Learn about different types of scoring system in performance assessment: holistic scoring, analytic scoring, primary-trait scoring, and multiple-trait scoring
2. Understand about the major concepts of scoring in objective tests: item facility and item discrimination
3. Create a scoring criteria for a specific test

Scoring of Performance-based Assessment

In the area of educational assessment, developing robust scoring systems for performance-based grading and classical objective testing is crucial. These systems must offer structured evaluation methods that accurately reflect learners' knowledge and skills. While classical objective testing often relies on quantifiable correct and incorrect answers, performance-based scoring emphasizes practical skills, application, and demonstrations of knowledge which makes it particularly relevant for language courses focused on speaking or writing. Performance-based scoring often involves qualitative assessments using descriptive feedback, ratings, or scores aligned with rubric criteria. The rubrics or assessment guidelines should be well-defined, and raters should be trained to ensure consistency. Analytic, holistic, primary-trait, and multiple-trait scoring are different approaches to evaluating performance in various assessments, such as writing, presentations, or performances. Each scoring system has distinct characteristics and is suited for different types of tasks.

Key Aspects of Performance-based Scoring:

- **Qualitative Assessments**: Performance-based scoring frequently employs qualitative assessments, utilizing descriptive feedback, ratings, or scores based on detailed rubric criteria.
- **Rubrics and Consistency**: The creation of clear, well-defined rubrics is essential. Additionally, rater training is imperative to ensure consistency and fairness in evaluation.
- **Scoring Approaches**: Various approaches, including analytic, holistic, primary-trait, and multiple-trait scoring, cater to different assessment objectives and contexts. Each system offers unique advantages for evaluating complex student performances.

Types of Scoring Methods

Now, let's see the definition and characteristics of each scoring method in the next section.

Holistic Scoring Approach

Holistic scoring involves assessing the overall performance or product as a whole, considering the task's overall quality and effectiveness. This approach is more straightforward and less time-consuming than analytic scoring, as it focuses on the general impression rather than specific components. Characteristics of holistic scoring include:

- **Overall Impression**: The entire performance is assessed as a single entity, considering its overall impact.
- **Quick Evaluation**: Requires less time and effort compared to analytic scoring since there are no individual criteria to evaluate.
- **General Feedback**: Provides feedback on overall strengths and weaknesses, without specific details on particular components.

Table 6.1

Example of Holistic Scoring Rubic for Persuasive Essay Task

Score	Description
5 Excellent	The essay demonstrates a deep understanding of the topic. The position is well-supported with strong evidence, insightful reasoning, and well-structured arguments. The writing is exceptionally clear, organized, and exhibits an advanced level of language proficiency.
4 Good	The essay effectively presents a clear position on the topic, supported by relevant examples and reasoning. Arguments are well-organized and coherent. The writing demonstrates proficiency in the language, with few errors.
3 Adequate	The essay presents a position and provides some supporting points, but the arguments may lack depth or coherence. The writing is mostly clear, with some minor language errors that do not impede understanding.
2 Limited	The essay's position and arguments are weak, with insufficient support. The writing may lack organization and coherence. Language errors are noticeable and may interfere with comprehension.
1 Weak	The essay's position and arguments are unclear or absent. The writing lacks organization and coherence. Significant language errors make the essay difficult to understand.

In a presentation assessment, the teacher considers the overall effectiveness of the presentation, including factors like content, delivery, visual aids, and audience engagement. The teacher provides a single score based on their overall impression of the presentation.

Analytic Scoring Approach

Analytic scoring involves breaking down the performance into specific components or criteria and evaluating each component separately. It allows teachers to provide detailed feedback for different aspects of the task. This method is commonly used in performance-based assessments and characteristics of analytic scoring include:

- **Criterion-based**: Each criterion or component is evaluated independently based on predefined rubrics or guidelines.
- **Detailed feedback**: Provides specific feedback for each criterion, highlighting strengths and weaknesses.
- **Complex tasks**: Suited for tasks with multiple dimensions or complex requirements.
- **Time-consuming**: Requires more time and effort from assessors to evaluate each criterion individually.

In a writing assessment, the criteria for evaluation could include grammar, organization, vocabulary, coherence, and creativity. Each criterion is assessed separately, and the final score is a combination of the scores obtained in each category.

Table 6.2

Example of Analytic Scoring Rubric for L2 Writing Task

Criteria	Excellent (5)	Good (4)	Adequate (3)	Developing (2)	Limited (1)
Content	Presents a clear and well-developed argument.	Presents a coherent argument.	Presents an argument, but lacks depth.	Argument is weak and lacking in support.	No clear argument or irrelevant content.
Organization	Demonstrates a well-structured and logical flow.	Mostly well-organized with some minor issues.	Organized but lacks clear transitions.	Disorganized with major issues in sequencing.	Poorly organized and difficult to follow.
Vocabulary Use	Employs a wide range of precise and varied words.	Uses a good variety of vocabulary appropriately.	Vocabulary is basic and somewhat repetitive.	Limited vocabulary, impacting expression.	Extremely limited vocabulary, hindering clarity.
Grammar	Exhibits consistently accurate and complex grammar.	Shows good control with minor errors.	Some errors, but communication is not affected.	Frequent errors impeding communication.	Numerous critical errors affecting clarity.
Mechanics	Virtually error-free with excellent punctuation.	Mostly correct with minor punctuation errors.	Some punctuation errors that do not distract.	Frequent punctuation errors, distracting reader.	Numerous distracting errors in mechanics.

Primary-trait Scoring Approach

Primary-trait scoring is one of the analytic scoring methods used in educational and psychological assessments. Analytic scoring is an approach to scoring performance tasks, such as essays, speeches, or other open-ended responses, in which specific aspects or dimensions of the performance are evaluated separately and assigned individual scores. Primary-trait scoring is a method of assessment that focuses on evaluating a single specific trait or dimension of a performance or product. It is a simplified approach that allows teachers to concentrate on a particular aspect or skill that is critical for the task at hand. By focusing on one primary-trait, the scoring process becomes more straightforward and efficient. This method is commonly used when there is a dominant characteristic that is of particular interest or importance in the assessment.

- **Focused evaluation**: The assessment is centered on one primary-trait, disregarding other aspects of the performance.
- **Clear criteria**: Well-defined criteria are established to evaluate the chosen primary-trait.
- **Efficient grading**: Scoring becomes more efficient as teachers only need to consider one specific aspect.
- **Task specificity**: Primary-trait scoring is most effective when the chosen trait is crucial to the task being evaluated.

Primary-trait scoring allocates a single score to a performance, but the scoring procedure is designed for each individual task, or class of tasks. Weigle (2002, p. 110) lists the components of a primary-trait scoring guide as follows:

- A description of the task
- A statement of the primary-trait (construct) to be measured
- A rating scale with level descriptors
- Samples of performance to illustrate each level
- Explanations of why each sample was graded in the way it was

Example of Primary-trait Scoring for a L2 Presentation Task

Here's an example of a primary-trait scoring criteria for a second language (L2) presentation task. In this example, the task is to give an oral presentation about a famous historical figure. The primary-trait being measured is "Content and Organization." The scoring criteria include a rating scale with level descriptors, samples of performance, and explanations for each level.

1. **Task description**: Give a 5-minute oral presentation about a famous historical figure of your choice. The presentation should include a clear introduction, main points about the figure's life and achievements, and a coherent conclusion.
2. **Primary-trait to be measured**: Content and Organization
3. **Rating scale with level descriptors**:

Level	Description
5 Excellent	Presentation is well-organized and demonstrates a deep understanding of the historical figure's life and contributions. Key points are presented logically, with seamless transitions.
4 Good	Presentation is organized and shows a solid understanding of the historical figure's impact. Key points are clear and transitions are mostly smooth.
3 Adequate	Presentation is somewhat organized and covers the main aspects of the historical figure. Key points are evident, but transitions may be abrupt.
2 Limited	Presentation lacks clear organization and may be missing some key details about the historical figure. Transitions are weak.
1 Weak	Presentation is disorganized and lacks coherent content. Main points are unclear or incorrect.

This primary-trait scoring criteria provides a clear and detailed framework for evaluating student performance in the L2 presentation task. It outlines the expectations for each level, provides detailed information based on content and organization.

Multiple-trait Scoring Approach

Multiple-trait scoring, also known as multivariate or multidimensional scoring, combines elements of both analytic and holistic scoring. It involves evaluating multiple criteria or traits independently (similar to analytic scoring) and then synthesizing the scores to provide an overall assessment (similar to holistic scoring). Characteristics of multiple-trait scoring include:

- **Comprehensive assessment**: Evaluates multiple-traits or dimensions, providing a comprehensive view of the performance.
- **Efficient feedback**: Offers specific feedback for each trait and an overall impression of the performance.
- **Balanced approach**: Strikes a balance between detailed analysis and overall assessment.

In assessing a student's cultural artwork, multiple-traits could include creativity, use of color, composition, technique, and originality. Each trait is evaluated independently, and then the scores are combined to give an overall assessment of the artwork's quality.

Scoring in Classical Objective Tests

Objective testing focuses on assessing a student's knowledge, understanding, and recall of factual information. This type of assessment usually involves multiple-choice questions, true/false statements, matching exercises, and other structured formats. The primary-goal is to measure a student's proficiency in a specific subject area. Common types of objective testing include: Multiple-choice questions, True/False questions, matching questions, fill-in-the-blank questions, short response questions.

Objective testing typically employs a scoring key or answer sheet, making grading efficient and less subject to interpretation. Each question is assigned a specific point value, and students' scores are tallied to calculate their final grade. When developing scoring systems for both performance-based grading and objective testing, it's essential to consider the learning objectives, align assessments with the curriculum, ensure fairness, and provide constructive feedback to help students improve their learning. Additionally, involving multiple raters (especially for performance-based grading) and conducting periodic evaluations of the scoring system's effectiveness can enhance its reliability and validity.

Item Facility and Item Discrimination

Item facility and item discrimination are two important concepts in the field of educational measurement, specifically in the context of test development and assessment. These concepts help to evaluate the quality and effectiveness of individual test items.

- **Item facility**: it is also known as item difficulty, is a measure that indicates the proportion or percentage of test-takers who answered a particular test item correctly. It provides insights into how easy or difficult an item is for the test-takers. To calculate the IF index, add up the number of students who correctly answered a particular item, and divide that sum by the total number of students who took the test. As a formula, it looks like this:

$$IF = \frac{Ncorrect}{Ntotal}$$

where Ncorrect = number of students answering correctly
Ntotal = number of students taking the test

The result of this formula is an item facility value that can range from 0.00 to 1.00 for different items. Teachers can interpret this value as the percentage of correct answers for a given item. For example, the correct interpretation for an IF index of .23 would be that 23% of the students correctly answered the item, explaining that the item with an IF of .23 would be a very difficult question because many more students missed it than answered it correctly. Conversely, an IF of .86 would indicate that 86% of the students answered correctly and the item with an IF of .86 seemed a very easy item. Test developers use item facility to assess the appropriateness of individual test items. Ideally, a well-constructed test should have a mix of easy, moderate, and difficult items to effectively differentiate between test-takers with varying levels of proficiency.

Table 6.3

Responses of Ten Test Items (15 students)

	Item 1	Item 2	Item 3	Item 4	Item 5	Item 6	Item 7	Item 8	Item 9	Item 10	Total
S1	1	1	1	1	1	1	1	1	1	1	10
S2	1	1	1	1	1	1	1	1	1	1	10
S3	1	1	1	1	0	1	1	1	1	1	9
S4	0	1	1	0	1	1	1	1	1	1	8
S5	1	1	1	0	1	1	1	0	0	1	7
S6	0	1	1	1	1	0	0	1	0	1	6
S7	1	1	1	0	1	0	1	1	0	0	6
S8	1	1	1	1	0	1	0	0	0	0	5
S9	1	0	1	1	1	0	0	1	0	0	5
S10	1	0	0	0	1	1	0	0	0	1	4
S11	1	0	1	0	1	0	0	0	0	1	4
S12	1	1	1	0	0	1	0	0	0	0	4
S13	1	0	0	0	0	0	1	0	0	0	2
S14	0	1	0	0	0	0	1	0	0	0	2
S15	0	0	0	0	0	0	0	1	0	0	1

- **Item discrimination (ID)**: it is a measure that evaluates how well a test item distinguishes between high-performing test-takers and low-performing test-takers. It provides insights into the ability of an item to discriminate between individuals with different levels of proficiency. The reason for identifying these two groups is that ID allows teachers to contrast the performance of the upper-group students on the test with that of the lower-group students. The process begins by determining which students had scores in the top group on the whole test and which had scores in the bottom group. To do this, begin by lining up the students' names, their individual item responses shown as Table 6.3, and total scores in descending orders. Such a high-to-low arrangement allows for quick determination of which students fall into the high- and low-scoring groups. The upper and lower groups are sometimes defined as the upper and lower third, or 33%. To do this, calculate the item facility (the IF discussed above) for the upper and lower groups separately for each item. The item discrimination index can be calculated using the following formula:

$$ID = IF_{upper} - IF_{lower}$$

where ID = item discrimination for an individual item
IF_{upper} = item facility for the upper group on the whole test
IF_{lower} = item facility for the lower group on the whole test

For example, in Table 6.3, the IF for the upper group on item 4 is 0.6, because 3 out of 5 upper group answered it correctly. At the same time, the IF for the lower group on that item is .00 because everyone in the lower group answered it incorrectly. I calculated the item discrimination index for this item by subtracting the IF for the lower group from the IF for the upper group and got an index of the contrasting performance of those students who scored high on the whole test with those who scored low. In this case, it turned out to be 0.6 ($ID = IF_{upper} - IF_{lower} = 0.6 - 0.00 = 0.6$). An item discrimination index of 1.00 is very good because it indicates the maximum contrast between the upper and lower groups of students-that is, all the high-scoring students answered correctly, and all the low-scoring students answered incorrectly. If the item discrimination index is positive, it indicates that the item effectively discriminates between high and low performers. Test-takers who scored higher on the overall test are more likely to answer the item correctly compared to those who scored lower. On the contrary, if the item discrimination index is negative or close to zero, it suggests that the item is not effectively distinguishing between high and low performers. High item discrimination is desirable as it helps identify and differentiate between individuals with varying levels of proficiency, contributing to the overall accuracy and effectiveness of the test. Item facility and item discrimination are crucial measures used to assess the quality of test items. Test developers use these measures to identify and retain effective items in a test and improve the overall validity and reliability of the assessment.

Ideal items in an NRT development project have an average IF of .50 and the highest available ID. These ideal items would be considered well-centered - that is, 50% answer correctly and 50% incorrectly. In reality, however, items rarely have an IF of exactly .50, so those that fall in a range between .30 and .70 are usually considered acceptable. Once those items that fall within the allowable range of IFs are identified, the items among them that have the highest ID indexes would be further selected for retention in the revised test. This process can help the teacher to retain only those items that are well-centered and discriminate well between the low- and the high-scoring students. Ebel (1979, p. 267) has suggested the following guidelines for making decisions based on ID:

Table 6.4

Guidelines for Making Decisions based on Item Analysis

ID index	Description
.40 and up	Very good items
.30 to .39	Reasonably good but possibly subject to improvement
.20 to .29	Marginal items, usually needing and being subject to improvement
Below .19	Poor items, to be rejected or improved by revision

EXERCISES

Match the following terms with the correct definitions. Terms may be used more than once.

1. holistic scoring	4. multiple-trait scoring
2. item facility	5. primary-trait scoring
3. analytic scoring	6. item discrimination

1. __________ is a measure that indicates the percentage or proportion of test-takers who answered a specific test item correctly.

2. In __________, specific aspect or dimension that is essential to the task being assessed are evaluated separately.

3. __________ is a measure that evaluates how effectively a test item distinguishes between high-performing and low-performing individuals or groups.

4. This __________ is advantageous for providing specific feedback to individuals, helping them identify areas for improvement.

5. __________ is an assessment approach where the overall quality of the performance is evaluated as a whole, without breaking it down into separate traits or dimensions.

6. It is a __________ where the performance is evaluated based on several traits or dimensions simultaneously and then combined individual trait scores into one score.

7. __________ involves evaluating the performance based on specific aspects or dimensions of the task separately.

UNIT 7.

Teacher-made Criterion-referenced Tests and Standardized Norm-referenced Tests

Key Points

In this unit you will be able to:

1. Learn about the characteristics of teacher-made criterion-referenced tests
2. Learn about the characteristics of standardized norm-referenced tests
3. Recognize the differences between teacher-made criterion-referenced and standardized norm-referenced tests

Introduction of the CRTs and NRTs

This unit explores the distinctions and applications of teacher-made criterion-referenced tests (CRTs) and standardized norm-referenced tests (NRTs). CRTs assess a learner's performance against specific criteria or learning standards, focusing on mastery of particular objectives. In contrast, NRTs compare a learner's performance to that of peers, ranking individuals within a broader context.

Teacher-Made Criterion-Referenced Tests:

• **Purpose and Design**: CRTs aim to provide feedback on specific learning

objectives. They are intimately connected to the curriculum and require substantial effort from educators to deliver meaningful feedback.
- **Feedback and Instructional Value**: Effective CRTs offer detailed feedback that guides both learners and instructors in addressing learning gaps and reinforcing strengths. The instructional value, as highlighted by Oller (1979, p. 52), lies in the test's ability to inform teaching strategies and learning interventions.

Standardized Norm-Referenced Tests:

- **Comparison and Ranking**: Unlike CRTs, NRTs are designed to rank learners by comparing their performance to a norm group, which can provide valuable insights into a learner's relative standing.
- **Scope and Application**: NRTs are often used in large-scale assessments and have implications beyond the classroom, influencing educational policy and resource allocation.

Teacher-Made Criterion-Referenced Tests

Criterion-referenced tests (CRTs) are a type of assessment that evaluates a student's performance based on specific predetermined criteria or learning standards. Unlike norm-referenced tests, which rank students in comparison to their peers, CRTs focus on measuring how well a student has mastered particular learning objectives or competencies. Criterion-referenced tests are designed to give test-takers feedback, usually in the form of grades, on specific course or lesson objectives. Classroom tests involving students in only one course and connected to a particular curriculum are typical of criterion-referenced testing. A good deal of time and effort on the part of the teacher (test administrator) is sometimes required to deliver useful, appropriate feedback to students, or what Oller (1979, p. 52) called instructional value. In a criterion-referenced test, the distribution of students scores across a continuum may be of little concern as long as the instrument assesses appropriate objectives (Brown & Hudson, 2000; Lynch & Davidson, 1994; Sadler, 2005). In language assessment, with an audience of classroom language teachers and teachers in training, and with its emphasis on classroom-based assessment as opposed to large-scale standardized testing, criterion-referenced testing is of more prominent interest than norm-referenced testing.

Teacher-made criterion-referenced tests play a crucial role in language assessment due to their many advantages and their alignment with specific learning objectives. In criterion-referenced testing, the assessment is designed to align closely with the content and skills covered in a specific curriculum or educational program. The test items are constructed in such a way that they directly assess the student's knowledge and proficiency in the targeted learning outcomes. Criterion-referenced tests are commonly used in educational settings to assess learners' knowledge and skills in various subjects, such as language arts, mathematics, science, and other academic areas. They are valuable tools for promoting learning and guiding instructional decision-making, as they provide a clear picture of how well students are mastering specific learning objectives. Here are some of the key reasons highlighting the importance of using teacher-made criterion-referenced tests in language assessment:

- **Alignment with learning objectives**: Teacher-made criterion-referenced tests can be designed to directly align with the language learning objectives of a specific curriculum or course. This ensures that the assessment focuses on the content and skills that students are expected to acquire, making the evaluation more meaningful and relevant.

- **Individualized assessment**: Teachers can customize criterion-referenced tests to suit the individual needs and abilities of their students. By tailoring the test items, teachers can better evaluate each student's progress and identify their strengths and areas needing improvement.
- **Assessment of specific language skills**: Language learning encompasses various skills such as reading, writing, listening, and speaking. Teacher-made criterion-referenced tests can isolate and assess specific language skills, allowing teachers to gain insights into the students' performance in each area.
- **Continuous monitoring of progress**: Since teachers create these tests, they have the flexibility to administer them at regular intervals, allowing for continuous monitoring of student progress throughout the academic year. This helps identify the growth and development of language skills over time.
- **Immediate feedback and intervention**: With criterion-referenced tests, teachers can promptly provide feedback to students about their performance. This enables timely interventions to address learning gaps and reinforce specific language skills as needed.
- **Diagnostic and formative assessment**: Criterion-referenced tests can be used for diagnostic purposes, helping teachers identify specific areas of difficulty for individual students or the entire class. This data can inform instructional strategies and curriculum adjustments to better meet students' needs.

Teacher-made criterion-referenced tests are valuable tools in language assessment, as they offer tailored evaluation of language skills, individualized feedback, and continuous monitoring of student progress.

They empower teachers to make informed instructional decisions and support students' language learning journey effectively. Using criterion-referenced assessment may provide better information about student achievement levels and mastery of academic objectives; however, the criterion-referenced test may not always adequately represent growth within a given curriculum. To more effectively measure student progress within a curriculum, teachers should rely on measures that use that curriculum, such as curriculum-based assessment and direct measurement. One difficulty that teachers may have in constructing criterion-referenced tests is establishing the exact criterion for whether the student has achieved the objective.

Example 1

Grammar Test

Objective: Evaluate students' understanding of a specific grammar concept, such as verb tenses.

Test Items: Choose the correct verb tense (past, present, future) for each sentence:

a) She ___________ (eat) breakfast every morning.
b) Yesterday, they ___________ (go) to the park.
c) By this time tomorrow, I ___________ (finish) my project.

Scoring: Each correctly chosen verb tense receives 1 point.

Criteria Level: Students should be able to identify and use the correct verb tense in sentences.

Example 2

Writing Task - Grammar Usage

Objective: Assess students' ability to use specific grammar rules in a given written task.

Test Item: Write a short paragraph about your last vacation, using a variety of verb tenses (past, present, future).

Scoring: The paragraph is scored based on the appropriate use of different verb tenses (e.g., past, present, future).

Mastery Criteria Level: Students will demonstrate mastery if they correctly apply the specified grammar rules in at least 80% of the sentences in their written response.

Non-Mastery Criteria Level: Students who correctly apply the specified grammar rules in fewer than 80% of the sentences will not achieve mastery.

In all these examples, the key aspect of criterion-referenced testing is that the assessment is aligned with specific learning objectives or criteria. Students' performance is evaluated based on their ability to meet those criteria, rather than being compared to the performance of their peers (as in norm-referenced testing). This approach provides a clear indication of each student's mastery of the targeted skills or knowledge.

Table 7.1

Most Common Task Errors of Test Construction

Test Format	Multiple-Choice Items
• Absence of directions • Answering procedures unclear • Items not consecutively numbered • Inadequate margins • Answer space not provided • No space between items	• Alternatives not in columns or rows • Incomplete stems • Negative words not emphasized or avoided • "All or none of above" not appropriately 0sed • Needless repetitions of alternatives • Verbal associations between alternative and stem
Matching Items	**True-False Items**
• Columns not titled • Response column not ordered • Directions do not specify basis for match • Answering procedures not specified • Columns exceed 10 items	• Statements contain more than a single idea • Negative statements used • Presence of a specific determiner • Needless phrases present, too lengthy
Completion Items	**Essay Exercises**
• Not complete interrogative sentence • Textbook statements with words left out • More than a single idea or answer called for • Question allows more than a single answer	• Response expectations unclear • Scoring points not realistically limited • Optional questions provided • Restricted question not provided • Ambiguous words used

Standardized Norm-Referenced Tests

Norm-referenced assessment in second language education is a type of standardized assessment that compares a student's performance to that of a representative group of students who have previously taken the same test. The purpose of norm-referenced assessment is to determine where a student's proficiency or performance level stands relative to the performance of others in the normative group. This type of assessment is commonly used to measure a learner's language proficiency or language-related skills in comparison to peers or a broader population. Norm-referenced tests are intended to be administered to large audiences, with results efficiently disseminated to test-takers. Such tests must have fixed, predetermined responses in a format that can be scored mechanically at minimum expense. Cost and efficiency are primary concerns in these tests.

Norm-referenced assessment does not measure absolute proficiency; instead, it focuses on comparing performance among test-takers. The test does not provide information about an individual's absolute language proficiency level, but rather their rank or position in comparison to others. So the results of the norm-referenced assessment allow educators and stakeholders to interpret a student's performance in relation to others in the norm group. For example, a student scoring in the 75th percentile performed better than 75% of the students in the norm group. Key features of norm-referenced assessment in L2 education include:

1. **Contents and Items**
   - **Sufficient Number of Items**: A language proficiency test should include a sufficient number of items to provide a reliable measure of an individual's proficiency. The exact number of items will depend on the purpose of the test and the time available for administration.
   - **Balanced Content Representation**: Ensure that the test items cover a balanced representation of the language skills being assessed. This typically includes listening, speaking, reading, and writing. Each skill area should have an appropriate proportion of items based on the overall test objectives.
   - **Item Difficulty Levels**: Include items that span a range of difficulty levels to effectively differentiate between individuals with varying

levels of proficiency. This ensures that the test can accurately capture the full spectrum of language abilities, from novice to advanced.

2. **Standardized Administration**: The test is administered under standardized conditions to ensure consistent administration and scoring across all test-takers.
3. **Norm Group**: The performance data collected from the representative sample forms the norm group. Descriptive statistics, such as mean, standard deviation, and percentile ranks, are calculated based on the norm group's performance.
4. **Percentile Scores**: Test-takers' scores are compared to the norm group's scores to determine their relative position within the reference group. A percentile score indicates the percentage of students in the norm group who scored at or below a particular test score.

It's important to note, however, that norm-referenced assessments have limitations. They may not capture the full range of language skills and abilities, and the reference group might not represent the entire population of language learners. As a result, norm-referenced assessments are often complemented with other assessment methods, such as criterion-referenced assessment, which focuses on measuring performance against predefined criteria or learning objectives. The examples of norm-referenced tests in L2 language education: These tests are often used for educational, occupational, or certification purposes and are scored based on a comparison with a representative sample of test-takers. Here's an overview of the purpose, characteristics, item types, and number of items for some well-known standardized norm-referenced language proficiency tests: TOEFL, TOEIC, and IELTS.

Table 7.2

Examples of Standardized Norm-referenced Tests

	TOEFL (Test of English as a Foreign Language)	TOEIC (Test of English for International Communication)	IELTS (International English Language Testing System)
Purpose	To assess the English language proficiency of non-native speakers who plan to study in an English-speaking environment. It measures reading, listening, speaking, and writing skills.	To assess English language proficiency in a business context, particularly focusing on listening and reading skills.	To evaluate the English language proficiency of individuals for academic, immigration, or employment purposes. It assesses reading, writing, listening, and speaking skills.
Characteristics	Available in both internet-based (iBT) and paper-based formats (less common). It features academic content and tasks to simulate the language skills required in an academic setting.	Mainly consists of multiple-choice questions that evaluate how well test takers understand and use English in various workplace scenarios.	Available in two versions: Academic and General Training. The Academic version is suitable for those applying to study in English-speaking countries, while the General Training version is often used for immigration and work purposes.
Item Types	Multiple-choice questions, integrated tasks (combining skills like reading & listening), and independent tasks (writing essays & speaking responses).	Listening comprehension questions (photographs, conversations, talks) and reading comprehension questions (business-related texts).	Multiple-choice questions, short answer questions, essays, graphs/charts interpretation, and a face-to-face speaking interview.
Number of Items	A total of 4 sections: Reading (30-40 questions), Listening (28-39 questions), Speaking (4 tasks), and Writing (2 tasks).	Listening and Reading test has a total of 200 questions (100 for listening and 100 for reading), divided into two sections.	The number of items in each section of the IELTS test may vary. For example, the IELTS Academic Writing section includes 2 tasks (150 and 250 words), while the IELTS Listening section has 4 parts.

These standardized tests are administered worldwide and serve as benchmarks for evaluating English language proficiency. The characteristics, item types, and number of items vary to assess different aspects of language skills and cater to various purposes, such as academic admission, employment, or immigration requirements.

EXERCISES

Match the following terms with the correct definitions. Terms may be used more than once.

1. norm-referenced test	4. evaluation criteria
2. feedback	5. learning objectives
3. criterion-referenced test	

1. In a teacher-made criterion-referenced test, the assessment focuses on evaluating students' mastery of specific learning objectives and standards. The test provides valuable ___________ for both teachers and students to measure individual progress.

2. A ___________ compares learners' performance to that of a normative group. The scores are presented in percentile ranks, which show how well a student performed compared to others who took the same test.

3. In a teacher-made criterion-referenced test, the ___________ are predefined and aligned with specific learning objectives. Each question is designed to assess students' understanding of particular academic concepts.

4. A standardized ___________ is often used for purposes such as college admissions or assessing program effectiveness.

5. The results of a ___________ provide detailed insights into each student's individual strengths and weaknesses.

6. A teacher-made criterion-referenced test is designed to assess students' mastery of specific ___________.

PART III

Assessing Language Ability

UNIT 8.

Assessing Listening

Key Points

In this unit you will be able to:

1. Understand the concept of listening ability
2. Learn about different types of listening skills: micro skills and macro skills
3. Recognize the importance of listening strategies: cognitive, metacognitive, socio-effective, interactive, task-based strategies
4. Create an effective listening task to assess L2 learners' listening ability

Introduction to Assessing L2 Learners' Listening Ability

Assessing listening skills in L2 learners is a multifaceted process that requires a balanced approach between formal and informal assessment methods. The choice of assessment techniques depends on various factors, including learner levels, assessment objectives, and available resources. A well-rounded assessment strategy begins with setting clear goals and choosing methods that accurately reflect learners' listening competencies.

Key Strategies for Listening Assessment

- **Establishing Goals and Objectives**: Defining what the assessment aims to measure is critical for selecting relevant assessment tools.
- **Formal Assessments**: Utilize structured approaches like multiple-choice

tests, gap-fill exercises, and dictation to quantify specific listening skills.
- **Informal Assessments**: Incorporate observations, group discussions, and self-assessments to provide a broader understanding of listening abilities.

How to Assess L2 learners' Listening Ability in the Classroom

Assessing L2 learners' listening ability in the classroom can be done through a variety of methods, including formal assessments and informal assessments. The specific methods for assessing L2 learners' listening ability may vary depending on the level of the learners, the goals and objectives of the assessment, and the resources available. It is, thus, important to choose appropriate methods and to understand the limitations and assumptions of the methods used. Effective assessment of listening abilities begins with the establishment of clear assessment goals and objectives, which serve as a guide for selecting appropriate methods. Formal assessments, such as multiple-choice tests, gap-fill exercises, and dictation, are employed to measure specific language skills. In addition, assessment flexibility is enhanced by incorporating informal methods, like teacher observations, group discussions, and one-on-one interviews. To evaluate learners' understanding in practical contexts, the assessment includes authentic materials, such as real-life conversations, news broadcasts, and lectures. Moreover, the assessment involves providing clear instructions and using diverse question types to assess main ideas, details, inferences, and opinions. Both accuracy and fluency in listening are evaluated, and learners are offered constructive feedback to support their future improvement. Multiple assessments are employed over time to gain a comprehensive view of learners' progress in listening comprehension.

Nature of L2 Listening Ability

Listening ability encompasses various types, each influenced by the context and purpose of listening. Some of the most common types include active listening, which involves paying full attention to the speaker and providing feedback to demonstrate understanding in interpersonal communication, counseling, and customer service. Critical listening, on the other hand, centers around evaluating communicated information, considering biases and perspectives, and making judgments about its quality and validity, often applied in academic and professional settings. Discriminative listening focuses on recognizing specific sounds or words, useful in language learning and situations requiring specific information. Comprehensive listening aims to understand the overall meaning and message, including main ideas, supporting details, and speaker's opinions, commonly found in academic and professional settings like lectures and presentations. Additionally, appreciative listening emerges in contexts of enjoyment and appreciation for artistic and emotional elements, such as music, storytelling, and poetry, relevant to entertainment and cultural contexts. Each type of listening ability requires different listening skills and strategies, and the specific type of listening ability required will depend on the context and purpose of the listening task. Effective listening requires the development and application of a range of listening skills, and it is important for listeners to be able to choose the appropriate type of listening ability for each situation.

Types of Listening Skills: Micro-skills and Macro-skills

Listening is a complex process that involves the comprehension and interpretation of spoken language. For L2 learners, listening is an essential skill that requires both micro skills and macro skills. Micro skills refer to the smaller, specific skills required for effective listening, such as recognizing individual words, understanding grammar, and identifying discourse markers. Macro skills refer to the larger, more general skills required for effective listening, such as understanding the main ideas and themes, making inferences, and evaluating the speaker's opinions and attitudes. According to Brown and Abeywickrama (2019), micro sckills includes skills to attend to the smaller bits and chunks of language, in more of bottom-up process while macro skills more focus on the larger elements involved in a top-down approach to a listening task.

Micro Skills

1. **Word recognition and speech delivery**
    - Discriminate among the distinctive sounds of English
    - Recognize individual words in spoken language,
    - Recognize reduced forms of words
    - Recognize English stress patterns, rhythmic structure, intonation
    - Process speech containing pauses, errors, corrections at a different rate

2. **Grammar recognition**
    - Recognize grammatical structures in spoken language
    - Recognize grammatical word classes (e.g., nouns, verbs), systems (e.g., tense, agreement, pluralization), patterns, rules, and elliptical

forms

- Distinguish word boundaries, recognize a core of words, and interpret word order patterns

3. Phrase recognition

- Recognize common phrases and expressions in spoken language
- Retain chunks of language of different lengths in short-term memory
- Detect sentence constituents and distinguish between major and minor constituents

4. Discourse marker recognition

- Recognize discourse markers, such as conjunctions that signal the relationship between ideas in spoken language
- Recognize cohesive devices in spoken discourse

Macro Skills

1. Understanding main ideas

- Comprehend the overall purpose and meaning of a spoken message
- Recognize the communicative functions of utterances according to situations, participants, and goals

2. Making inferences

- Infer situations, participants, and goals using real-world knowledge
- Predict outcomes, infer links and connections between events, deduce causes and effects, and draw conclusions based on information that is not directly stated in spoken language
- Distinguish between literal and implied meanings

3. Evaluating speaker's opinions and attitudes
- Understand and interpret the speaker's opinions, attitudes, and emotions in spoken language.

4. Interpreting nonverbal cues
- Understand and interpret nonverbal cues, such as body language and tone of voice, in spoken language
- Use facial, kinetic, and body language, and other nonverbal clues, to decipher meanings

(Adapted from Brown & Abeywickrama, 2019)

In order to effectively develop L2 learners' listening skills, it is essential to address both the micro skills and macro skills in language instruction and assessment. This requires a balanced approach that includes opportunities for learners to practice listening to a variety of authentic materials and to receive feedback on their listening ability.

Types of L2 Listening Strategies

It is worth noting that the developments in L2 listening strategies are an ongoing and dynamic research area. Language educators and researchers continually explore and refine these strategies to optimize language learning outcomes for students. Some common types of L2 listening strategies include metacognitive strategies, cognitive strategies, socio-affective strategies, interactive strategies, task-based strategies.

- **Cognitive listening strategies**: Cognitive strategies refer to techniques that learners use to understand and process the incoming auditory information

(Goh, 2017). These strategies aim to enhance learners' memory, attention, and cognitive processing abilities during listening activities. An L2 learner might employ a cognitive strategy by predicting what information they expect to hear next based on the context and prior knowledge. This prediction helps them anticipate the content and focus their attention accordingly.

- **Metacognitive listening strategies**: Researchers (i.e., Vandergrift, 2007; Vandergrift & Goh, 2012) have been focusing on metacognitive strategies, which involve learners' awareness and control of their listening process. These strategies help learners monitor their comprehension, set goals, and evaluate their understanding during listening tasks. For example, the L2 learner uses self-monitoring techniques during the listening task to check understanding and adjust their comprehension strategies accordingly.
- **Socio-affective listening strategies**: Socio-affective strategies involve learners' attitudes, beliefs, and social interactions during the listening process (MacIntyre et al., 2011). These strategies recognize the importance of motivation, self-confidence, and interaction with others in improving listening comprehension. For example, an L2 learner might use a socio-affective strategy by engaging in conversations with native speakers or fellow learners to practice listening in real-life situations, which can boost their confidence and motivation to improve their listening skills.
- **Interactive listening strategies**: As language learning has increasingly become technology-driven, interactive strategies that involve the use of digital tools and platforms have gained attention. These strategies leverage technology to provide learners with interactive listening exercises, immediate feedback, and personalized learning experiences (Wang, 2020). An L2 learner might use language learning apps or online platforms that provide interactive listening exercises and instant feedback. An interactive

listening platform might present learners with videos or audio clips and prompt them to answer questions or participate in interactive quizzes to reinforce their listening skills.

- **Task-based listening strategies**: Recent research (i.e., Ellis, 2003) has focused on task-based language learning, where listening activities are integrated into meaningful tasks. These strategies emphasize the importance of context and authentic language use for enhancing listening comprehension. In a task-based listening activity, L2 learners might listen to an authentic interview and then complete a task like summarizing the main points, identifying specific information, or participating in a role-play based on the content of the interview.

Developing effective L2 listening strategies involves a combination of self-awareness, practice, and targeted approaches (Field, 2008; Godwin-Jones, 2019; Graham et al., 2008; Rost, 2014; Thorne & Reinhardt, 2008; Vandergrift & Goh, 2012; Vandergrift & Tafaghodtari, 2010). Developing effective L2 listening strategies involves self-assessment and goal setting. It is important for L2 learners to assess their current listening skills in the target language, identifying strengths and weaknesses, and set specific and achievable listening goals that align with their language learning objectives. To enhance listening skills, they should regularly expose themselves to authentic materials such as podcasts, news broadcasts, interviews, and movies in the target language. Starting with materials slightly above their current level can challenge them while still being manageable. Engaging in active listening practice by focusing on specific aspects, like identifying main ideas, details, or specific information, and using techniques such as predicting, summarizing, and questioning, can improve comprehension. During listening tasks, L2 learners benefit from taking notes to reinforce understanding, using symbols, abbreviations, and short phrases for efficiency. Additionally, they can utilize technology by using language learning apps, online exercises, and interactive platforms that offer targeted listening practice, making the most of multimedia resources with audio and video components for an immersive experience. Finally, reflecting on their progress regularly and adapting their listening strategies as needed, while acknowledging that language learning is a gradual process requiring patience, is essential for success.

How to Design an Effective Listening Task for L2 Learners

Designing effective listening tasks for L2 learners requires careful consideration of the type of listening task, the level of the learners, the goals and objectives of the task, and the resources available. In designing effective listening tasks, teachers need to consider the following guidelines. Firstly, they should use authentic materials that reflect real-life language use, such as news broadcasts, podcasts, and real-life conversations in audio or video recordings. Secondly, teachers need to select listening tasks appropriate for the learners' level, considering their language proficiency, vocabulary, and grammatical knowledge. Thirdly, clear and concise instructions for the listening task, including the task type, purpose, and expectations for learners, should be provided. Fourthly, pre-listening activities, like previewing vocabulary or asking prediction questions, can help learners prepare for the task and increase motivation. Fifthly, post-listening activities, such as summarizing main ideas or evaluating the speaker's opinions, are important to reinforce comprehension and interpretation. Additionally, teachers should offer opportunities for feedback, providing both positive and constructive feedback to learners.

Lastly, a balanced approach between intensive, extensive, and interactive listening experiences ensures a comprehensive learning approach.

It is crucial for teachers to choose appropriate methods based on learners' levels, goals, objectives, and available resources while being aware of the limitations and assumptions of the methods used. When designing L2 listening test items, it's essential to consider the language proficiency level of the learners and ensure the audio recordings are of high quality and appropriately paced. Additionally, the test items should reflect real-life situations and topics relevant to the learners' language learning journey.

Developing Multiple-choice Items

Multiple-choice listening items involve presenting learners with a question or a prompt, followed by a set of options. Learners must listen to the audio and choose the correct option among the given choices.

Example

Prompt: Listen to the audio and choose the correct option.
Audio: "What did Sarah do last weekend?"
Options: a) Went shopping. b) Watched a movie.
c) Visited her grandparents. d) Played soccer.

Developing Short Response Items

Short answer listening items require learners to listen to the audio and provide a brief response, usually consisting of a word or a few words.

Example

Prompt: Listen to the audio and answer the question in a few words.
Audio: "What is the name of the main character in the story?"
Answer: ___________ (e.g., "John")

Developing Filling-in-the-gap Items

Gap filling listening items involve presenting learners with a text or sentence with some words missing. Learners must listen to the audio and fill in the missing words in the correct places.

Example

Prompt: Listen to the audio and complete the sentences with the missing words.
Audio: "My favorite subject in school is history. I love learning about science and science."
Sentence: "My favorite subject in school is ___________. I love learning about ___________ and ___________."
Answer: history, science

Developing Information Transfer Items

Information transfer listening items serve to evaluate learners' capacity to extract specific information from an audio source and convey it to another format, like completing a table, drawing a chart, or plotting routes on a map. The use of charts, maps, grids, timetables, and other real-life artifacts in these tasks enhances their authenticity, reflecting practical application in daily life situations.

Example 1

Prompt: Listen to the audio and complete the table with the relevant information.

Audio: "You will hear descriptions of different fruits. Complete the table."

Fruit	Color	Taste
Apple	Red	Sweet
Banana	________	________
Orange	________	Sour

Example 2

Prompt: Test-takers see:

Audio: a) A confident woman is giving a presentation.

b) The whiteboard displays four printed graphs.

c) Four people attentively listen to the presentation.

d) There are four cups of coffee and a glass jar.

Developing Dictation Items

Dictation listening items involve learners engaging in an audio passage and transcribing what they hear. This type of item serves to assess the learners' ability to comprehend spoken language accurately and reproduce it in writing. Dicto-comp and dictogloss are both pedagogical techniques used in language learning classrooms, particularly for assessing learners' listening ability. They are designed to improve learners' listening comprehension, grammar, vocabulary, and overall language proficiency by engaging them with authentic linguistic input. Here's a detailed description of each technique with examples.

- **Dicto-comp (dictation-composition):** Dicto-Comp is a teaching technique where the teacher dictates a passage to the students, who listen and take notes. After the dictation, students work individually or in groups to reconstruct the text as accurately as possible. This method emphasizes understanding and processing the content, vocabulary, and grammatical structures within the passage.

Example

In a language learning class, the teacher dictates a short story about a market visit, including descriptions of the market environment, interactions with shopkeepers, and items bought. After the dictation, students are asked to write their version of the story using their notes. The activity concludes with a comparison of the learners' texts with the original, discussing vocabulary, grammar, and comprehension.

- **Dictogloss**: Dictogloss is a more collaborative and interactive approach than Dicto-comp task. In this method, the teacher reads a short, authentic text aloud at normal speed, and students listen without taking notes. After a first listening, students note down what they can remember. The teacher reads the text again, and students add to their notes. Finally, in pairs or small groups, students reconstruct the text to the best of their ability. The focus is on the gist, key vocabulary, and grammatical structures. The teacher facilitates a discussion, comparing the reconstructed texts with the original. This task not only help learners improve their language skills but also encourage active listening, collaboration, and critical thinking. They are adaptable to various proficiency levels and can be used to focus on different linguistic elements depending on the learning objectives.

Example

For a dictogloss activity, the instructor selects a passage about environmental conservation. After listening to the passage twice, learners work in groups to reconstruct the text, focusing on the main ideas and specific language used to describe conservation efforts. The activity encourages discussions about language use, grammar, and the importance of listening for key information.

EXERCISES

Match the following terms with the correct definitions. Terms may be used more than once.

1. proficiency	3. multiple-choice item
2. short response item	4. gap-filling

1. One effective way to assess listening skills is to have students complete a __________ item where they fill in the missing words or phrases from a recorded conversation.

2. When designing listening assessment tasks, it is crucial to align the level of difficulty with the __________ of the students to ensure a fair evaluation.

3. To evaluate listening skills, teachers can use a __________ where students select the correct answer from a set of options based on what they heard.

4. To promote active listening, teachers can incorporate a __________ where students respond to questions or complete tasks based on what they heard.

UNIT 9.

Assessing Reading

Key Points

In this unit you will be able to:

1. Understand the concept of reading ability
2. Learn about L2 learners' reading process: Top-down, bottom-up, interactive reading process
3. Learn about different types of reading skills and strategies
4. Create an effective reading task to assess L2 learners' reading ability

Introduction to Assessing L2 Learners' Reading Ability

Unit 9 delves into the intricacies of assessing reading abilities in L2 learners, underscoring the enduring significance of the written word across various facets of life. Despite the proliferation of visual and auditory media, reading maintains a pivotal role in communication and learning. This unit emphasizes the need for effective assessment strategies to gauge learners' reading skills accurately, reflecting on the presumption of effortless acquisition of reading abilities in language education.

Key Concepts in Reading Assessment

- **Importance of Reading**: Reading is fundamental for academic success and effective communication in literate societies. It is often assumed that learners will naturally acquire reading skills, a notion that underscores the necessity for targeted assessment.

- **Assessment Strategies**: Evaluating reading ability requires a multifaceted approach, incorporating both direct measures of reading comprehension and indirect assessments that infer understanding through related tasks.

How to Assess L2 Learners' Reading Ability in the Classroom

Visual and auditory media have experienced rapid advancements due to technological progress, yet the written word continues to play a crucial role in communication, entertainment, and preserving social, economic, and legal conventions. In literate societies, children typically learn to read by the age of five or six, and for most, reading becomes a skill taken for granted. Similarly, in foreign language learning, teachers often expect learners to acquire reading abilities effortlessly. Beginning-level textbooks in foreign languages assume students' reading proficiency, given that a book serves as the medium. Many formal language tests use written texts to prompt responses, and even oral interviews may require reading for specific tasks. Reading remains a paramount skill in assessing general language ability, arguably being the most crucial for success in all educational contexts (Brown & Abeywickrama, 2019).

Bottom-up processing and top-down processing are two essential cognitive processes involved in reading tasks. These processes work together to enable efficient and effective reading comprehension. First, bottom-up processing is a data-driven approach to reading, where the reader starts with individual elements, such as letters and words, and builds up to construct meaning. In this process, the reader processes the text's smaller details and combines them to understand the larger context. Bottom-up processing is especially critical for beginning readers or when encountering unfamiliar words. It allows readers to build a foundation for understanding the text and gradually improve their reading skills. Top-down processing, on the other hand, is a conceptually driven approach to reading, where the reader draws on prior knowledge, experiences, and expectations to comprehend the text. In this process, the reader brings their background knowledge and context to interpret the meaning of the text. Top-down processing is beneficial for fluent readers who can use their existing knowledge and context to grasp the overall meaning of the text efficiently. It allows readers to engage with the text actively and apply their comprehension skills effectively. Here's how top-down and bottom-up processing works:

<u>Bottom-up reading process</u>

- **Letter and word recognition**: The reader identifies individual letters and words present in the text.
- **Phonics and decoding**: The reader applies phonics and decoding skills to pronounce and understand unfamiliar words based on the letter-sound relationships.
- **Syntactic parsing**: The reader processes the sentence structure and grammar to comprehend the order and arrangement of words.
- **Comprehending meaning**: By combining the recognized letters, words, and grammar, the reader assembles the information to understand the overall meaning of the text.

<u>Top-down reading process</u>

- **Activating background knowledge**: The reader accesses their prior knowledge about the topic or subject matter of the text.

- **Making predictions**: Based on the context and prior knowledge, the reader makes predictions about what they expect to find in the text.
- **Filling in gaps**: As the reader progresses through the text, they actively fill in gaps in their understanding based on their predictions and background knowledge.
- **Confirming or adjusting Understanding**: The reader constantly checks whether their predictions align with the information in the text. If discrepancies are found, the reader adjusts their understanding accordingly.

Additionally, the interactive reading process in L2 refers to the dynamic and reciprocal relationship between the reader and the text during the act of reading. It involves the active engagement of the reader with the language and content of the text to construct meaning and comprehend the information presented. The process is interactive because the reader constantly interacts with the text, drawing on various linguistic, cognitive, and metacognitive skills. The interactive reading process is dynamic and individualized, as each reader brings unique experiences, linguistic abilities, and cognitive processes to the task. It is a fundamental aspect of language learning, allowing learners to navigate authentic texts and develop their language proficiency in meaningful and contextually rich ways. Interactive reading in L2 involves a combination of cognitive processes, language skills, and personal experiences to actively engage with the text, comprehend its meaning, and make connections with prior knowledge and cultural contexts. The interactive nature of the reading process enables learners to deepen their understanding and build their language proficiency in a meaningful and contextually relevant way. Here is how interactive reading process works;

<u>Interactive reading process</u>

- **Activating background knowledge & using bottom-up processing**: The reader activates their prior knowledge related to the topic, genre, or cultural context of the text. This helps create a framework for understanding and connects new information to what they already know Then the reader starts decoding the text at the word and sentence level, using their knowledge of letters, words, grammar, and syntax. This bottom-up processing aids in recognizing individual words and understanding the basic structure of the sentences.
- **Implementing top-down processing**: Simultaneously, the reader employs top-down processing by using their background knowledge and context to make predictions, infer meanings, and anticipate the content. They rely on their prior knowledge to make sense of the text as a whole.
- **Monitoring comprehension**: Throughout the reading process, the reader continually monitors their understanding. They check if their predictions and inferences align with the new information encountered in the text.
- **Adjusting reading strategies & responding to the text**: If comprehension breaks down, the reader adjusts their reading strategies. They may re-read, use context clues, or consult additional resources to resolve any difficulties. After reading, the reader may engage in various post-reading activities, such as summarizing, discussing, or writing about the content. These activities reinforce comprehension and encourage critical thinking. The interactive reading process is continuous, as the reader actively engages with the text from the beginning to the end. It involves an ongoing interaction between the reader and the content.

Indeed, the reading processes of bottom-up, top-down, and interactive are not mutually exclusive, but rather complementary and interconnected.

Skilled readers seamlessly combine these processes during reading tasks, utilizing their knowledge of letters, words, and grammar (bottom-up) while drawing on their background knowledge and context (top-down) to achieve comprehensive reading comprehension. The interaction with the reading texts helps them obtain a deeper understanding of the content, allowing for a more meaningful and enriching reading experience. As readers advance in their skills, they become more adept at integrating these processes, leading to enhanced reading abilities. This integration allows readers to construct meaning from the text efficiently and effectively, making connections between different elements of the reading process to achieve a deeper understanding of the content. Ultimately, a balanced approach that combines bottom-up, top-down, and interactive reading processes is essential for successful L2 reading and language proficiency development.

Types of Reading Skills: Micro-skills and Macro-skills

Micro skills and macro skills are two different types of reading skills that are used to comprehend written text. Micro skills refer to the small, specific skills that an L2 reader uses to understand individual words, phrases, and sentences. Macro skills refer to the larger, overarching skills that a reader uses to understand the overall structure and meaning of a text. Both micro and macro skills are important for effective reading and play a role in determining a reader's overall reading ability. Effective readers use a combination of both types of skills to understand and evaluate written text, and it is important for L2 learners to develop both their micro and macro reading skills in order to become successful and confident readers in their second language.

Micro Skills

1. **Vocabulary**: Understanding the meanings of words and their relationships with other words.
   - Discriminate among the distinctive graphemes (letters or letter combinations that produce a phoneme) and orthographic patterns of English
2. **Decoding**: Recognizing and decoding individual words and phrases.
3. **Grammar**: grammatical word classes (nouns, verbs, etc.)
   - Recognize a core of words and interpret word order patterns and their significance
   - Recognize grammatical word classes (nouns, verbs, etc.), systems (e.g., tense, agreement, pluralization), patterns, rules, and elliptical forms
   - Recognize that a particular meaning may be expressed in different grammatical forms
4. **Fluency & accuracy**: Reading with speed, accuracy, and expression.
   - Process texts at an efficient rate of speed to suit the purpose
5. **Comprehension**: Understanding the meaning of individual words, phrases, and sentences.
   - Recognize cohesive devices in written discourse and their role in signaling the relations between and among clauses

Macro Skills

1. **Summarizing**: Condensing the main ideas and details of a text into a shorter form.
   - Recognize the rhetorical conventions of written discourse and their significance for interpretation
2. **Analyzing**: Breaking down the structure and components of a text and examining how they contribute to the overall meaning.

   • Distinguish between literal and implied meanings

3. **Inferencing:** From described events, ideas, and so on, infer links and connections between events, deduce causes and effects, and detect such relations as main idea, supporting idea, new information, given information, generalization, and exemplification
   • Infer context that is not explicit using background knowledge
   • Develop and use a battery of reading strategies, such as scanning and skimming, guessing the meaning of words from context, and activating schemata to interpret texts
4. **Evaluating:** Making judgments about the quality, validity, and relevance of information presented in a text.
   • Detect culturally specific references and interpret them in a context of the appropriate cultural schemata

Types of Reading Strategies

The assessment of reading can imply the assessment of a storehouse of reading strategies. Aside from simply testing the ultimate achievement of comprehension of a written text, it may be important in some contexts to assess one or more specific reading strategies. The following brief taxonomy of strategies is a list of possible assessment criteria. L2 reading strategies are techniques and approaches used by language learners to comprehend and process written texts in L2. These L2 reading strategies are essential tools that help learners effectively comprehend and engage with written texts in a second language. By employing a combination of these strategies, language learners can enhance their reading skills and overall language proficiency. These strategies includes as following.

- **Skimming**: it involving quickly glancing over the text to get a general idea of the main topic or theme. For example, reading the headlines and first paragraphs of a news article can be part of skimming to understand the main story.
- **Scanning**: it includes rapidly searching the text for specific information or keywords. Looking for dates, names, or numbers in a text without reading it fully is an example of scanning strategy.
- **Predicting**: it involves making educated guesses about the content based on the title, subheadings, or prior knowledge. Predicting the possible outcome of a story is an example of prediction strategy.
- **Guessing from context**: Inferring the meaning of unknown words or phrases based on the surrounding context. Understanding the meaning of a word by looking at how it is used in the sentence is an example of using context clues.
- **Identifying text structure**: Recognizing the organization of the text, such as headings, paragraphs, and bullet points, to aid comprehension. Understanding the sequence of events in a narrative by identifying paragraphs is an example of using text structure to aid comprehension.
- **Recognizing cohesive devices**: Identifying cohesive devices, like pronouns and connectors, to understand how ideas are connected. Using discourse markers (e.g., in addition, however, nevertheless) to process relations can be part of the cohesive devices strategy.
- **Inferencing**: Drawing conclusions and making educated guesses about implicit information in the text. Understanding a character's feelings or motivations based on their actions is an example of using inferencing as part of the reading strategy.
- **Summarizing**: Briefly restating the main points or ideas of a text in one's own words. Writing a concise summary of a news article after

reading it is an example of using summarizing as a reading strategy.

- **Support strategies**: Use marginal notes, outlines, charts, or semantic maps to understand and retain information. Note-taking while reading can be helpful to highlight key information and reinforce understanding.

How to Design an Effective Reading Task for L2 Learners

L2 reading assessment tasks can vary in their format and purpose, aiming to evaluate different aspects of learners' reading abilities. Here are some types of L2 reading assessment tasks, along with examples of each task item:

Developing Multiple-choice Questions

Multiple-choice questions are a common type of assessment task where learners are presented with a question or a statement, and they must choose the correct answer from a set of options. These questions assess various reading skills, such as understanding main ideas, identifying details, making inferences, and evaluating the author's tone or purpose. Multiple-choice questions provide a range of possible answers, including distractors that may seem plausible but are incorrect. Learners need to carefully analyze the options and select the most accurate response based on their comprehension of the text.

Example

Read the passage and choose the best answer to the question:

> Dolphins are highly intelligent marine mammals known for their playful behavior. They are social creatures that live in groups called pods. Dolphins

communicate using a variety of clicks and whistles. These sounds help them locate food, navigate, and stay in touch with other pod members.

What is the main purpose of the clicks and whistles dolphins produce?
A) To scare away predators
B) To communicate with humans
C) To find food and navigate
D) To establish dominance within pods

Activity: Developing Reading Comprehension Items

Create reading comprehension questions that assess main ideas, details, and inferential understanding based on the following short passage.

The Galápagos Islands, located about 1,000 kilometers west of Ecuador in the Pacific Ocean, are renowned for their unique biodiversity. These islands became famous after Charles Darwin visited them in 1835, which contributed significantly to the development of his theory of evolution by natural selection. The Galápagos are home to species found nowhere else on Earth, such as the giant Galápagos tortoises, marine iguanas, and the flightless cormorants. The isolation of the islands has led to the development of these species' unique adaptations, making the Galápagos a living laboratory for scientists studying evolution and conservation. Despite their remote location, the Galápagos Islands face threats from tourism, invasive species, and climate change, challenging conservationists to balance human interests with the preservation of the islands' natural heritage.

Developing Short Response Items

Short answer questions require learners to provide brief and precise responses to specific prompts or questions. These questions assess the ability to recall information, understand key points, and demonstrate knowledge of the content. Learners must formulate concise answers without elaborating excessively. Short answer questions can also assess critical thinking skills, as learners may need to justify their responses or support their answers with evidence from the text.

Example

- What are the three main reasons the author gives to support their argument in the text?
- Who was the author of the book mentioned in the passage?

Developing Fill-in-the-blanks Items

Fill in the blanks items present a text with certain words or phrases omitted. Learners are required to fill in the missing information using appropriate words or phrases. This type of task assesses vocabulary knowledge, grammatical accuracy, and contextual understanding. It also measures how well learners can predict words based on the context of the sentence or paragraph.

Developing Sequencing Items

Sequencing tasks involve arranging a series of events, ideas, or sentences in the correct chronological or logical order. These tasks assess learners' ability to understand the overall structure and coherence of a text. They require learners to analyze the relationships between different parts of the text and demonstrate comprehension of the sequence of events or ideas presented in the reading passage.

Example

Sequencing Events in a Story

Read the following sentences and put them in the correct order to form a coherent story.

1. One sunny morning, Tom woke up early and decided to go for a walk in the park. The birds were singing, and the flowers were blooming.
2. As he walked along the path, Tom noticed a stray dog wandering around. It looked hungry and lost. Tom felt bad for the dog and decided to take it home.
3. When Tom arrived home, he fed the dog and gave it some water. The dog wagged its tail and seemed grateful.
4. The next day, Tom put up posters around the neighborhood, hoping to find the dog's owner. He also took the dog to the local animal shelter to check for a microchip.
5. After a few days, no one claimed the dog, and Tom decided to adopt it. He named the dog Lucky and they became best friends.

Developing Critical Reading Items

Critical reading test items go beyond simple comprehension and assess higher-order thinking skills. These items often require learners to analyze, interpret, and evaluate the text critically. They may involve tasks such as writing a summary, making connections between the text and real-life situations, identifying the author's bias or perspective, or expressing personal opinions based on the reading. Critical reading test items measure learners' ability to think critically about the content and apply their knowledge and understanding in a thoughtful and analytical manner.

Example 1

Write a paragraph expressing your opinion on the author's argument in the text, providing reasons to support your viewpoint.

Example 2

Analyze the character's actions and motivations in the story and explain how they contribute to the plot.

Developing Information Transfer Items

Information transfer items in L2 reading testing assess learners' ability to extract specific information from a given text and transfer it to another format or context. These tasks require learners to comprehend the content thoroughly and accurately convey the relevant information in a different form. Information transfer items aim to evaluate not only reading comprehension but also the learners' ability to apply the acquired knowledge and use language in a purposeful manner.

Example

"Meet the Animal Kingdom!"

Let's learn about some fascinating animals from around the world:

1. African Elephant: The African Elephant is the largest land mammal,

with long tusks and distinctive ears. It mainly inhabits the savannas and forests of Africa.

2. Bengal Tiger: The Bengal Tiger is a majestic big cat with striking orange fur and black stripes. It can be found in the forests of India and Bangladesh.
3. Arctic Fox: The Arctic Fox has a thick white fur coat that helps it survive in cold Arctic regions. It is well-adapted to its snowy habitat.
4. Green Sea Turtle: The Green Sea Turtle is a marine reptile that navigates through the oceans, and it is known for its herbivorous diet and beautiful green skin.
5. Red-eyed Tree Frog: The Red-eyed Tree Frog is a vibrant amphibian found in the rainforest of Central and South America. Its bright red eyes are a striking feature.

Now, let's fill in the chart with some information about these animals:

Animal Habitat	Habitat	Distinctive Feature
African Elephant		
Bengal Tiger		
Arctic Fox		
Green Sea Turtle		
Red-eyed Tree Frog		

Developing Matching Items

Matching tasks in L2 reading testing require learners to match items from one list to corresponding items in another list based on information presented in the text. These tasks assess learners' ability to identify relationships, make connections, and demonstrate comprehension of the content. Matching tasks at a sophisticated level for L2 learners may involve discerning pragmatic interpretations of certain signs or labels. Matching tasks in L2 reading testing are versatile and can be used to assess various types of knowledge and comprehension, such as vocabulary, factual information, cause-effect relationships, and more. These tasks require learners to carefully read and understand the text, make connections between different pieces of information, and demonstrate their ability to apply their knowledge effectively.

Example

Match Signs to Their Pragmatic Interpretations

List A: Signs or Labels

"No Shirt, No Shoes, No Service"
"Keep Off the Grass"
"Reserved Parking"
"Quiet Please"

List B: Pragmatic Interpretations

a. This area is designated for special guests or permit holders only.
b. Please maintain silence in this area to avoid disturbing others.
c. To enter this establishment, you must be dressed appropriately with a shirt and shoes.
d. Do not step or walk on the grass in this area.

Developing Cloze Test Items

The cloze task has been widely used as a reading assessment tool. In this task, a sentence with a missing word is presented to the reader, and they are expected to fill in the gap with a calculated guess based on context, linguistic expectancies, background experience, and strategic competence. Cloze procedure is most commonly associated with reading only. The cloze test consists of a passage in which every nth word (typically every seventh word) is deleted and the test-taker is asked to supply an appropriate word in its generic form,. Some research on SLA supports cloze testing as an integrative measure of not only reading ability but also other language skills, such as listening, speaking, and writing (Brown, 2002; Jonz, 1991; Oller & Jonz, 1994; Watanabe & Koyama, 2008). However, with the decline in the search for the ideal integrative test, cloze testing is now recognized as one of many assessment procedures available to test reading ability(Greene, 2001). Cloze tests typically consist of at least two paragraphs to account for discourse expectancies. Designing cloze tests involves choosing deletions and scoring criteria carefully. Deletions can be made at fixed intervals or rationally based on grammatical or discourse functions, allowing designers to avoid difficult-to-predict words.

Example

Cloze Test (Fixed-ratio deletion - every seventh word)

The sun was shining brightly in (1)__________ clear blue sky. The children were (2)__________ happily in the park, laughing and (3)__________ around. Suddenly, dark clouds appeared, and (4)__________ began to rain. The children ran for (5)__________ as the rain poured down.

Cloze Test (Rational Deletion)

The sun was shining (1)__________ in the clear blue sky. The children were playing (2)__________ in the park, laughing and running around. (3)__________, dark clouds appeared, and it began to rain. The children ran for cover as the rain poured down.

EXERCISES

Match the following terms with the correct definitions. Terms may be used more than once.

1. sentence	6. top-down
2. holistic	7. bottom-up
3. word-level	8. macro reading skill
4. micro reading skills	9. interactive
5. metacognitive	10. schema

1. To improve ___________, learners need to focus on enhancing their word recognition and expanding their vocabulary. On the other hand, developing ___________ involves practicing longer texts, identifying main ideas, and making connections between paragraphs.

2. One key strength of the bottom-up process is its emphasis on ___________ accuracy and decoding skills.

3. Readers using the bottom-up approach pay close attention to grammar and ___________ structures to derive meaning.

4. In the ___________ reading process, readers start by processing individual elements, such as letters and phonemes, and then build up to understanding larger units of text.

5. The ___________ reading process involves readers using their background knowledge and context to anticipate and predict the content of the text.

6. Readers who approach text from a top-down perspective often engage in ___________ reading, focusing on the overall meaning rather than individual words.

7. In the top-down reading process, readers use their __________ and experiences to make educated guesses about unfamiliar words.

8. The __________ approach places importance on overall comprehension and understanding rather than word-by-word decoding.

9. The __________ process combines both bottom-up and top-down strategies to construct meaning from the text.

10. Readers who employ the interactive approach are more likely to develop __________ reading skills, which are essential for comprehension.

UNIT 10.

Assessing Speaking

Key Points

In this unit you will be able to:

1. Understand the concept of speaking ability
2. Learn about L2 learners' speaking process: Top-down, bottom-up, interactive reading process
3. Learn about different types of speaking skills and strategies
4. Create an effective speaking task to assess L2 learners' speaking ability

Introduction to L2 Speaking Ability Assessment

This unit explores the multifaceted nature of speaking ability in L2, emphasizing the importance of assessing a learner's capacity to communicate effectively in the target language. Speaking assessments are designed to evaluate various aspects of language production, including pronunciation, grammar, vocabulary, fluency, and interactional skills, through diverse tasks like speaking tests, oral presentations, and role-plays.

Key Components of Speaking Assessment

- **Nature of Speaking**: Speaking in L2 encompasses the ability to use language dynamically to express ideas, opinions, and feelings across different contexts.

- **Assessment Tasks**: Effective speaking assessments employ tasks that mimic real-life communication, such as interviews, discussions, and simulations, to gauge authentic language use.
- **Skills Evaluated**: A comprehensive speaking assessment covers pronunciation, grammatical accuracy, lexical range, fluency, and the ability to engage in interactive communication.

Nature of L2 Speaking Ability

The nature of speaking ability in L2 refers to a learner's ability to communicate effectively and fluently in the target language. This refers to a learner's ability to produce language, that is, to use language to express ideas, opinions, and feelings in a variety of contexts. This type of speaking ability is often assessed through tasks such as speaking tests, oral presentations, or role-plays. It encompasses several different aspects of language use, including pronunciation, grammar, vocabulary, fluency, and interactional skills. From a pragmatic perspective on language performance, listening and speaking skills are often closely interconnected. In real-world situations, language skills are usually integrated in various combinations. While it is theoretically possible to isolate some listening tasks, it is challenging to separate oral production tasks from aural comprehension completely. Only in specific speaking contexts, such as monologues, speeches, or reading aloud, can we assess oral language without the direct participation of an interlocutor. However, even in these situations, the test-taker's listening ability inevitably influences their oral production, which can compromise the reliability and validity of oral production tests.

Another challenge lies in designing elicitation techniques for oral language assessment. Since speaking involves creative construction, test-takers make choices regarding vocabulary, sentence structure, and discourse. To assess specific spoken grammatical categories, the stimulus must be carefully designed to prevent test-takers from avoiding or paraphrasing and to encourage the production of the target form. Open-ended test tasks pose a greater scoring challenge due to the test-taker's freedom of choice. In receptive performance, the elicitation stimulus can anticipate predetermined responses, but in productive performance, the stimulus must be specific enough to elicit outputs within an expected range for appropriate scoring or rating procedures.

For example, in a picture-series task aimed at eliciting a story in a sequence of events, test-takers might provide various plausible ways to tell the story, all of which could be equally accurate. Evaluating such diverse responses becomes a challenge. One possible solution is to assign multiple scores for each response, with each score representing one of several traits, such as pronunciation, fluency, vocabulary use, grammar, and comprehensibility. In summary, when assessing oral production, the interrelated nature of listening and speaking skills must be considered, and elicitation techniques should be carefully designed to ensure targeted and reliable assessment of the test-taker's language abilities. Multiple scoring traits may be employed to comprehensively evaluate the complex nature of oral language performance (Brown & Abeywickrama, 2019).

Types of Speaking Skills: Micro-skills and Macro-skills

Assessing speaking ability in L2 involves evaluating both micro skills and macro skills. These terms refer to specific components of language proficiency that contribute to an individual's overall speaking competency. Micro skills are fundamental building blocks, and improving them can lead to enhanced speaking proficiency. These are the smaller, more specific language skills that are involved in speaking, such as pronunciation, grammar, and vocabulary. They include the ability to produce accurate sounds, stress, and intonation patterns in the target language, as well as to use appropriate grammar structures and vocabulary.

Macro skills are broader, higher-order language abilities that involve more extended and complex communication. These skills are typically evident in more extended speech, such as conversations or presentations. These are the larger, more global aspects of language use that involve the use of language in context, such as fluency, coherence, and interactional skills. They include the ability to speak smoothly and efficiently, to organize ideas and information into a logical and coherent message, and to use language appropriately in different social and cultural contexts. Let's explore each skill category:

<u>Micro Skills</u>

1. Phonetics & Pronunciation
   - Articulate sounds, stress, intonation, and rhythm accurately in the L2.
   - Understanding and correctly using the sounds of the L2.
   - Produce English stress patterns, words in stressed and unstressed positions, rhythmic structure, and intonation contours
   - Produce differences among English phonemes and allophones

2. Vocabulary
   - Use words and phrases in the target language appropriately
   - Use an adequate number of lexical units (words) to accomplish pragmatic purposes

- Produce reduced forms of words and phrases

3. Grammar
   - Exhibit mastery of sentence structure, verb tenses, word order, and other grammatical features.
   - Use grammatical word classes (nouns, verbs, etc.), systems (e.g., tense, agreement, pluralization), word order, patterns, rules, and elliptical forms
   - Express a particular meaning in different grammatical forms

4. Fluency
   - Produce smooth and natural flow of speech, without significant pauses or hesitations.
   - Produce fluent speech at different rates of delivery
   - Deliver speech using natural phrasing, appropriate pauses, sentence structures

5. Discourse markers
   - Use words or phrases to organize speech, signal transitions, or emphasize points (e.g., "first of all," "however," "in conclusion").
   - Use cohesive devices in spoken discourse

<u>Macro Skills</u>

1. Communicative competence
   - Use language effectively in real-life communication situations, considering sociolinguistic and cultural factors.
   - Appropriately accomplish communicative functions according to situations, participants, and goals

2. Cohesion & Coherence
   - Create a well-structured and connected discourse, where ideas are organized logically.

- Convey links and connections between events and communicate such relations as focal and peripheral ideas, events and feelings, new information and given information, generalization, and exemplification

3. Negotiation of meaning
    - Clarify and modify communication when faced with misunderstandings or communication breakdowns.
4. Extensive vocabulary use
    - Utilize a diverse range of words and expressions to convey specific meanings.
5. Contextual appropriateness
    - Use language appropriately based on the situation, audience, and purpose.
    - Convey facial features, kinesics, body language, and other nonverbal cues along with verbal language
6. Interactive communication
    - Engage in conversation, actively participating, and responding to others effectively.
    - Use appropriate styles, registers, implicature, redundancies, pragmatic conventions, conversation rules, floor-keeping and floor-yielding, interrupting, and other sociolinguistic features in face-to-face conversations
7. Strategy use
    - Monitor ones own oral production and use various strategies: emphasizing key words, rephrasing, providing a context for interpreting the meaning of words, appealing for help, using pauses, fillers, self-corrections, backtracking to enhance the clarity of the message

Assessment of L2 speaking ability often involves evaluating both micro skills and macro skills. Evaluators may use various techniques, such as interviews, oral presentations, role-plays, and discussions to assess these aspects of language proficiency. Providing constructive feedback on both micro skills and macro skills can guide learners towards improving their overall speaking ability in the second language.

How to Design an Effective Speaking Task for L2 Learners

There are three main types of speaking tasks in an L2 classroom: intensive, extensive, and interactive speaking tasks. Each type of task focuses on different aspects of speaking ability and provides different opportunities for learners to practice and develop their speaking skills.

Intensive Speaking Task

Intensive speaking tasks focus on specific language skills, such as pronunciation, grammar, and vocabulary. They are often used to provide targeted practice for learners and to help them develop their micro speaking skills.

Pronunciation Drills or Exercises: Pronunciation drills aim to enhance learners' ability to articulate sounds and intonation patterns accurately. These exercises often involve repetitive practice and focus on specific phonemes or aspects of pronunciation.

Example

Minimal Pairs Practice

The teacher presents pairs of words that differ by one sound, and the learner must correctly identify and produce the words. For instance:

- Ship / Sheep
- Bet / Bat
- Heat / Hit

Picture-cued Elicitation Task: The picture-cued elicitation task in L2 speaking assessment involves using visual stimuli (pictures or images) to prompt learners to talk about future events or actions. This task aims to assess the learner's ability to use the future tense correctly and express themselves fluently in the target language. The pictures serve as triggers for conversation, allowing learners to construct sentences and narratives about what they see.

Example

Task Instructions: The examiner provides the learner with a set of pictures that depict various future scenarios or situations. The learner is then asked to describe what they see in the pictures, making predictions, discussing future plans, or imagining potential outcomes.

Example Pictures:

Test-takers hear: A group of people sitting at a table with party decorations.
Prompt: "Describe what you think is happening in this picture and what might happen in the future."

1. The assessor points to the picture in general: what are these people doing?
2. The assessor points to the kid who enjoys his birthday party: What will the boy do next?
3. The assessor points to the girl next to the boy. what is she going to do there?

Read Aloud Task: The read aloud task in L2 speaking assessment is designed to evaluate a learner's ability to read written text out loud in the target language. This task assesses various aspects of their speaking proficiency, including pronunciation, intonation, fluency, and comprehension. Here's how the read aloud task works, along with example tasks for different proficiency levels:

Example

Task Instructions:

The examiner provides the learner with a written passage or text in the target language. The length and complexity of the text depend on the learner's proficiency level. Before beginning the task, the examiner may give some brief instructions, such as asking the learner to read clearly and at a natural pace.

Beginner Level:

Text: "My name is Emily. I am ten years old. I live in a small town near the mountains. I go to school every day and play with my friends in the park. Today, I am going to the zoo with my family."

Responsive Speaking Tasks

Responsive speaking tasks in L2 speaking assessment aim to evaluate a learner's ability to interact with prompts and produce appropriate responses in real-time. Two common responsive tasks are the question and answer task and paraphrasing task. Let's explore each with examples:

Short Response Task: In this task, the examiner asks the learner a series of questions, and the learner must respond to each question with relevant answers. This task assesses the learner's ability to comprehend and respond appropriately to different types of questions.

Example

Questions:

a. What did you do last weekend?

b. How do you usually travel to work or school?

c. Can you tell me about your favorite book or movie?

d. What are your plans for the upcoming holidays?

The learner's responses are evaluated based on the following criteria:

- Clarity and coherence of answers
- Grammatical accuracy
- Vocabulary use
- Pronunciation and fluency

- **Paraphrasing Task**: In the paraphrasing task, the examiner presents a sentence or short text, and the learner must rephrase or explain the content using different words or expressions while retaining the original meaning. This task assesses the learner's language flexibility and ability to communicate effectively.

Example

Test-taker hear: Paraphrase the following text in your own words.

Once upon a time, there was a brave knight named Arthur. He lived in a kingdom ruled by a wise king. One day, a ferocious dragon attacked the kingdom, causing fear among the people. Arthur decided to face the dragon and protect his kingdom. With his shining armor and a mighty sword, he rode his horse towards the dragon's lair. After a fierce battle, he defeated the dragon and saved the kingdom. The people celebrated his bravery, and he became a legendary hero.

Test-taker respond with two or three sentences.

The test-taker's paraphrasing is evaluated based on the following criteria:
- Accuracy in conveying the original meaning
- Use of different vocabulary and sentence structures
- Grammatical correctness

Utilizing such tasks provides several advantages, as they encourage test-takers to generate succinct responses, potentially accessing their conversational ability to be concise. When using short paraphrasing tasks for assessment, it becomes essential to clarify the task's objective. In this context, the emphasis is likely on integrating listening and speaking skills rather than solely evaluating oral production. Both of these responsive speaking tasks offer valuable insights into the learner's ability to engage in spontaneous conversations and demonstrate language proficiency in real-life situations. By assessing the learner's performance in these tasks, instructors can provide targeted feedback to help learners improve their speaking skills and gain confidence in using the target language effectively.

Interactive Speaking Tasks

Interactive speaking tasks are designed to engage learners in active communication with others, simulating real-life language use and promoting fluency, negotiation of meaning, and critical thinking. Here are examples of different interactive speaking tasks:

• **Oral Interview**: In an oral interview, a learner interacts with an examiner or interviewer who asks questions on various topics. The learner responds to the questions, showcasing their ability to communicate effectively in the target language. An effective interview includes the essential stages of an effective interview for oral proficiency testing proposed by Canale (1984). The interview consists of four stages:

Figure 10.1

Four Stages of Oral Interview

Step 1. Warm-up	This initial stage involves a short period of small talk to introduce the test-taker to the situation and format, easing any anxieties. It is not scored.
Step 2. Level check	The interviewer uses preplanned questions to gauge the test-taker's proficiency level, asking questions based on their expected language abilities. The responses are scored, and the interviewer aims to confirm the assumed proficiency level.
Step 3. Probe	In this stage, the interviewer challenges the test-taker with more difficult questions to assess the upper limits of their language proficiency. The complexity of the probe questions increases as the test-taker responds.
Step 4. Wind-down	The final stage is a brief period to relax the test-taker with easy questions and provide information on obtaining the interview results. This phase is not scored.

Questions are usually designed to elicit grammatical categories (such as past tense or subject-verb agreement), discourse structure (a sequence of events), vocabulary usage, and/or sociolinguistic factors (politeness conventions, formal/informal style, etc.)

Example

Oral Interview about Travel Experiences

Step 1: Warm-up

Interviewer: "Hello! Welcome to the interview. Could you please introduce yourself and tell me a bit about your travel experiences?"

Step 2: Level Check

Interviewer: "Great! Now, I'd like to know more about your recent trip. Can you describe the last place you visited and share your impressions of it?"

Step 3: Probe

Interviewer: "You mentioned you visited a historical city. Could you elaborate on the historical landmarks you saw there and their significance?"/"Imagine you're planning your next trip. What factors would you consider when choosing your destination?"

Step 4: Wind-down

Interviewer: "Thank you for sharing your travel experiences with us. Before we finish, let's talk about something fun. If you could travel anywhere in the world, where would you go and why?"/"It was a pleasure talking with you today. Do you have any questions for me about the interview process or when you'll receive your results?"

- **Role Play**: Role play involves learners assuming different roles and engaging in simulated conversations or scenarios. This task allows learners to practice using language in specific contexts. In certain instances, role play offers students the opportunity for rehearsal, allowing them to plan and prepare their responses beforehand. Additionally, it can alleviate anxieties as students briefly adopt the persona of someone else, offering a momentary escape from their own identities (Oradee, 2012). Role play, as an assessment tool, offers unique opportunities for test-takers to engage in discourse that might otherwise be challenging to elicit. Various personal, strategic, and linguistic aspects of learners' oral abilities come to the forefront. While the interviewer can guide or control the role play, this technique allows test-takers to showcase creativity and complexity similar to real-world pragmatics. Scoring, however, poses typical challenges found in tasks with somewhat unpredictable responses. The test administrator must define the assessment objectives of the role play and devise a scoring technique that effectively captures these objectives.

Activity: Role-play Scenarios

Instructions for Students:
You will participate in role-play scenarios designed to use specific grammar structures and vocabulary. Each scenario is based on everyday situations where you will have to interact using the target language points. Focus on applying the grammar and vocabulary accurately while also striving for fluency and coherence in your conversations.

1. Preparation
    - **Review Target Grammar and Vocabulary:** Before the role-play, students should review the specific grammar structures and vocabulary expected to be used in the scenarios.
    - **Role Assignment:** Each student will be assigned a role that comes with a brief description of their character's background and objectives within the conversation.
    - **Scenario Context:** Each scenario is outlined with a specific context and

objectives for each participant.

2. Examples of Role-play Scenarios

(1) Making a Hotel Reservation

- **Grammar Focus**: Future tense, modal verbs for requests (e.g., could, would).
- **Vocabulary Focus**: Accommodation types, amenities, booking terms.
- **Roles**: Customer and Hotel Receptionist.
- **Context**: The customer is trying to book a room for their upcoming vacation, asking about prices, availability, and hotel services.

(2) Ordering Food in a Restaurant

- **Grammar Focus**: Present continuous tense for immediate decisions, quantifiers (e.g., some, any, much, many).
- **Vocabulary Focus**: Types of food, expressions for preferences and dietary restrictions.
- **Roles**: Customer and Waiter/Waitress.
- **Context**: The customer is at a restaurant, deciding what to order. They ask about menu recommendations, specify dietary preferences, and inquire about dish ingredients.

(3) Planning a Weekend Trip

- **Grammar Focus**: Use of "going to" for future plans, comparative and superlative adjectives.
- **Vocabulary Focus**: Travel destinations, activities, and transportation.
- **Roles**: Two Friends.
- **Context**: The friends are discussing where to go for a weekend trip, comparing different places and activities, and deciding on travel arrangements.

3. Guidelines for Effective Role-play

- **Stay in Character**: Try to embody your role fully, responding as you believe your character would in the given situation.
- **Use Target Language Points**: Focus on incorporating the grammar structures and vocabulary relevant to the scenario.
- **Listen and Respond**: Engage actively with your partner's contributions,

showing understanding and building on the conversation.

4. Assessment Criteria

Criteria	Description
Accuracy	Use of correct grammar and vocabulary
Fluency	Ability to communicate ideas smoothly and without significant hesitation
Coherence	Logical flow of conversation and relevance of contributions
Interactive Competence	Effectiveness in initiating and responding to dialogue, including turn–taking and negotiation of meaning

- **Discussions and Conversations**: In discussions and conversations, learners interact with each other or with the teacher to exchange ideas, opinions, and information on various topics. As informal techniques for assessing learners, discussions and conversation tasks offer a level of authenticity and spontaneity that other assessment methods may lack. As formal assessment tools, however, these speaking tasks involving groups of students present challenges in terms of specification and scoring (May, 2011; Nakatsuhara, 2011). Discussions can be particularly suitable for eliciting and observing various abilities, such as: Topic nomination, maintenance, and termination, attention-getting, clarifying, questioning, and paraphrasing, or negotiating meaning, etc. When assessing learners' performance using scores or checklists, it's essential to carefully design them to align with the observed discussion's objectives. However, teachers should be cautious about using checklists, as they may induce anxiety in students, potentially negatively affecting their performance. Another challenge lies in the integrative nature of discussions, warranting the evaluation of learners' comprehension alongside their production.

Example

Teacher: "Discuss the advantages and disadvantages of social media."

- Learner 1: "Well, one advantage is that it helps us stay connected with friends and family."
- Learner 2: "True, but it can also be a distraction and lead to privacy concerns."

- **Information Gap Activities:** Information gap activities involve learners working in pairs or groups, where each participant has different information. They must exchange information to complete a task or solve a problem. The information transfer task is a valuable component of L2 speaking assessment as it tests the learner's comprehension of visual data and their capacity to present it orally in a well-organized manner. It also assesses their ability to communicate effectively in real-life situations where they may need to interpret and convey information from charts, graphs, or other visual aids.

Example

Task Instructions:

1. The examiner provides the learner with visual information, such as a chart, graph, or picture, containing data or details related to a specific topic.
2. The learner is given a short amount of time (usually a minute or two) to study the visual information and understand its content.
3. The examiner then instructs the learner to orally convey the information from the visual aid in the form of spoken language, providing a concise summary or description.

4. The learner should communicate the key points and relevant details from the visual information accurately and clearly, without reading directly from the chart or graph.

▌Student A Family Members

	Relationship	Personality	Job	Birth
Ken		funny	teacher	
Sarah	aunt			1982
Mia	sister			
Alex		reliable	lawyer	2005

▌Student B Family Members

	Relationship	Personality	Job	Birth
Ken	grandfather			1953
Sarah		friendly	doctor	
Mia		serious	mechanic	1990
Alex	cousin			

Assessment Criteria: The learner's performance in the information transfer task is evaluated based on the following criteria:

- Accuracy in conveying the information from the visual aid.
- Clarity and coherence in spoken language.
- Ability to summarize key points concisely.
- Correct use of appropriate vocabulary and language structures.

Interactive speaking tasks are dynamic and create an authentic language environment. They encourage learners to use language in context, negotiate meaning, and build confidence in their communication skills. These tasks are excellent tools for assessing and improving speaking proficiency in the target language.

EXERCISES

Match the following terms with the correct definitions. Terms may be used more than once.

1. micro skills	4. interactive
2. speaking ability	5. intensive
3. macro skills	6. responsive

1. ___________ speaking tasks are designed to improve speaking accuracy and fluency by drilling and practicing specific language elements.

2. ___________ skills in speaking refer to the precise use of individual sounds, words, and grammar to ensure clarity and accuracy. On the other hand, ___________ skills involve organizing ideas, using cohesive devices, and maintaining coherence during longer stretches of speech.

3. ___________ tasks focus on enhancing learners' ability to express themselves naturally in various situations.

4. ___________ allows learners to share their thoughts, feelings, and experiences with others. It is a learnable skill that requires practice and feedback to improve fluency and accuracy.

5. The primary goal of ___________ speaking tasks is to foster authentic communication and encourage active participation.

6. ___________ speaking tasks focus on developing specific language features, such as pronunciation, intonation, and vocabulary usage.

7. Learners participating in ___________ tasks must provide immediate answers based on their understanding of the topic.

8. __________ tasks promote interpersonal communication skills as learners actively listen, respond, and engage in meaningful conversations.

UNIT 11.

Assessing Writing

Key Points

In this unit you will be able to:

1. Understand the nature of writing ability in L2
2. Learn about different types of writing skills and strategies
3. Create an effective writing task to assess L2 learners' writing ability

Introduction to L2 Writing Ability Assessment

Unit 11 delves into the multifaceted process of assessing writing in a second language (L2), highlighting the complexity of determining the specific constructs to be evaluated. Writing assessment encompasses a broad spectrum of skills, from handwriting and spelling to grammar, coherence, and logical argumentation. This unit underscores the intrinsic link between writing and reading, as effective writing presupposes the ability to read and understand one's own text.

Key Components of Writing Assessment

- **Writing Constructs**: Identifying and assessing various aspects of writing, including mechanical skills (handwriting, spelling) and higher-order skills (coherence, argument development).
- **Integration with Reading Skills**: Recognizing the interdependence of

reading and writing in the assessment process, where comprehension of prompts is crucial for a meaningful response.

Nature of L2 Writing Ability

The assessment of writing is a complex task that requires clarity regarding the specific construct or ability being tested. Various aspects of writing can be assessed, such as handwriting ability, correct spelling, grammatically sound sentences, coherent paragraph construction, and logical development of main ideas. Each of these constructs can be evaluated through different tasks, providing a comprehensive picture of a student's writing skills. It is essential to recognize that assessing writing also inherently involves the assessment of reading. One cannot write a sentence in a language without the ability to read the sentence just written. Therefore, the testing of writing ability is closely interconnected with reading skills. Most writing assessment tasks rely on written or oral prompts, and test-takers need to comprehend these prompts to respond effectively. Hence, assessing writing is typically integrated with another language skill, highlighting the interdependence of various language abilities in communication and written expression. (Brown & Abeywickrama, 2019).

Writing ability in L2 refers to a learner's ability to produce written texts in the target language. Writing ability is a complex and multifaceted skill that involves the mastery of a range of micro and macro skills, such as grammar, vocabulary, fluency, coherence, and organization. L2 writing ability is shaped by a number of factors, including a learner's language proficiency, their familiarity with the target culture and discourse conventions, and their background knowledge and experience. Effective L2 writing requires not only the ability to produce grammatically correct sentences, but also the ability to use appropriate vocabulary, to organize ideas and information effectively, and to engage with the reader in a meaningful and appropriate way.

In an L2 language classroom, the development of writing ability is an important goal, as it provides learners with a valuable tool for communication and for demonstrating their language proficiency. Effective L2 writing instruction should aim to build learners' writing skills through focused practice and feedback, as well as by providing opportunities for learners to engage with authentic texts and to use writing for communicative purposes.

In recent L2 writing instruction, there has been a significant emphasis on both the process-based approach and genre-based approaches. These approaches aim to create a comprehensive framework for teaching writing that incorporates both the writing process and the study of writing genres. The process-based approach, for instance, guides learners through various stages of writing, including prewriting, drafting, revising, editing, and publishing. L2 writers are encouraged to explore their own writing style and freely express their ideas. They receive valuable feedback on their writing, which encourages them to revise and improve their work. Additionally, this approach encourages L2 writers to reflect on their writing process and employ effective strategies to enhance their writing skills.

The genre-based approach is characterized by the analysis of various writing genres, including narratives, reports, essays, and job-related writing, etc, to comprehend their structure, language features, and purposes. By doing so, L2 writers are equipped with the conventions and norms specific to each genre, enabling them to write effectively within its boundaries. This approach emphasizes writing in specific contexts, aiding L2 learners in producing texts suitable for various communicative situations. Moreover, L2 writers engage in the analysis of authentic texts from diverse genres, gaining valuable insights into effective writing techniques and strategies.

In the context of L2 writing assessment, recent approaches aim to evaluate both the writing process and the ability to produce texts effectively in different genres. Process-based writing assessments concentrate on evaluating learners' proficiency in the writing process, encompassing prewriting, drafting, revising, and editing. These assessments observe learners' writing performance to generating ideas, organizing content, and refining their work. Conversely, genre-based writing assessments focus on appraising learners' capacity to write in specific genres. L2 learners may be asked to produce texts that adhere to the conventions of different genres, demonstrating their understanding of structure, language features, and communicative purposes. Sometimes, L2 writing assessments may combine elements from both approaches, where learners go through the writing process while producing a particular genre of text. Overall, the integration of both process-based and genre-based writing approaches provides learners with a well-rounded foundation for writing proficiency and assessment. It enables them to develop writing skills through a structured process while acquiring the necessary knowledge and abilities to write effectively in diverse genres and contexts, fostering their versatility and competence as writers in their target language.

Types of Writing Genres

In L2 writing assessment, learners may be asked to perform one or multiple types of writing tasks to demonstrate their writing abilities in various contexts. The assessment may include formal tests, timed writing assignments, portfolios of written work, or collaborative writing tasks. Assessing different types of writing allows educators to evaluate learners' language development, creativity, critical thinking skills, and ability to communicate effectively in the target language. It also provides learners with opportunities to develop a range of writing skills necessary for various academic, professional, and real-life situations. Types of writing genres commonly evaluated in L2 writing assessment include:

- **Narrative writing:** Involves storytelling and recounting events or experiences in a coherent and engaging manner.
- **Expository writing:** Focuses on providing information, explanations, or instructions to the reader. Examples include reports, essays, and informative articles.
- **Persuasive writing:** Aims to convince the reader to adopt the writer's viewpoint or take specific action. It includes opinion pieces, argumentative essays, and persuasive letters.
- **Descriptive writing:** Focuses on vividly describing people, places, objects, or events using sensory details and imagery.
- **Creative writing:** Involves imaginative and expressive writing, such as poetry, short stories, or fictional dialogues.
- **Job-related writing**
  - Letter or Email Writing: Requires composing formal or informal letters or emails for specific communicative purposes.
  - Messages, memorandum, reports, schedules, labels, signs, advertisements, announcements, manuals

Types of Writing Skills: Micro-skills, Macro-skills, and Writing Strategies

The L2 writing skills can be broadly categorized into two categories: micro skills and macro skills. Micro skills pertain to the fundamental building blocks or individual elements of written language, whereas macro skills are vital for successfully mastering the required components of written language.

<u>Micro Skills</u>

1. **Grammar**
    - Use appropriate grammar structures in writing.
    - Use acceptable grammatical systems (e.g., tense, agreement, pluralization), patterns, and rules
    - Express a particular meaning in different grammatical forms
2. **Vocabulary**
    - Cover the range and accuracy of words used in writing.
    - Produce an acceptable core of words and use appropriate word order patterns
3. **Spelling**
    - Spell words correctly in writing
    - Produce graphemes and orthographic patterns of English
4. **Punctuation**
    - Use correct punctuation marks in writing.
5. **Sentence structure**
    - Write clear and coherent sentences.
    - Produce writing at an efficient rate of speed to suit the purpose

- Use cohesive devices in written discourse

<u>Macro Skills</u>

1. Cohesion

- Compose an assigned task by organizing the text in a manner that establishes clear connections and a logical flow of ideas

2. Coherence

- Compose an assigned task in a way that demonstrates clear organization, enabling readers to easily follow the writer's ideas.
- Use the rhetorical forms and conventions of written discourse

3. Paragraphing

- Divide the text into clear and coherent paragraphs.

4. Discourse organization

- Create the writing task, adhering to the overall organization of the text, which includes the introduction, body, and conclusion.
- Appropriately accomplish the communicative functions of written texts according to form and purpose
- Convey links and connections between events and communicate such relations as main idea, supporting idea, new information, given information, generalization, and exemplification

5. Register

- Effectively compose an assigned task by employing an appropriate tone, style, and level of formality in the writing, tailored to suit the specific audience and purpose.
- Correctly convey culturally specific references in the context of the written text

6. **Strategy development**

- Develop and use a battery of writing strategies, such as accurately assessing the audiences interpretation, using prewriting devices, writing with fluency in the first drafts, using paraphrases and synonyms, asking peer and instructor feedback, and applying feedback when revising and editing

Effective writing strategies encompass a range of techniques that can enhance the clarity, coherence, and persuasiveness of written communication. Some key types of effective writing strategies include:

Effective Writing Strategies

- **Planning and outlining:** Careful planning and creating a structured outline before starting to write can help organize thoughts and ensure a logical flow of ideas in the final piece.
- **Audience awareness:** Considering the intended audience while writing allows the writer to tailor the content, tone, and style to resonate with the readers' interests and needs.
- **Clear and concise language:** Using clear and straightforward language helps convey the intended message efficiently, avoiding ambiguity or confusion.
- **Varied sentence structure:** Employing a mix of sentence structures, including simple, compound, and complex sentences, adds variety and rhythm to the writing.
- **Transitions and cohesion:** Utilizing transitional words and phrases helps create smooth connections between ideas, ensuring coherence throughout the text.
- **Active voice:** Using the active voice makes writing more engaging and direct, placing the focus on the subject performing the action.

- **Proofreading and editing:** Taking the time to revise and edit the work for grammar, spelling, punctuation, and overall coherence ensures a polished and error-free final product.
- **Supporting evidence:** Backing up arguments and claims with relevant evidence and examples strengthens the persuasiveness of the writing.
- **Eliminating redundancy:** Avoiding unnecessary repetition and redundant phrases helps maintain clarity and conciseness.
- **Revision and feedback:** Revisiting and revising the initial draft based on feedback from peers or instructors can lead to improved content and overall effectiveness.

By employing these effective writing strategies, writers can create impactful and compelling pieces that effectively communicate their intended message to their target audience.

How to Design an Effective Writing Task for L2 Learners

In L2 writing instruction, three primary types of writing tasks exist, varying based on the extent of teacher intervention or learner engagement: controlled writing, guided writing, and free writing.

- **Controlled writing:** Controlled writing tasks are typically structured, repetitive exercises that focus on specific language features or structures. They are designed to help L2 writers improve their accuracy and fluency in using language structures and conventions. Examples of controlled writing tasks include sentence completion exercises, fill-in-the-blank tasks, and sentence transformation exercises.

- **Guided writing:** Guided writing tasks provide a more open-ended format for L2 writers, but still offer a clear structure and purpose. They provide more flexibility and creativity for L2 writers, while still focusing on specific language features or structures. Examples of guided writing tasks include writing a paragraph based on a prompt, writing a letter to a friend, or writing a description of a picture.
- **Free writing:** Free writing tasks allow for the greatest level of creativity and freedom for L2 writers. They usually do not have a specific structure or format and allow L2 writers to explore their own ideas and thoughts in writing. Examples of free writing tasks include journal writing, creative writing, and personal narratives.

Each type of writing task has its own advantages and disadvantages, and L2 writing teachers should consider the purpose and goals of the writing task when choosing the type of task to use in their instruction. It is important to incorporate a mix of controlled, guided, and free writing tasks in an L2 writing class in order to provide a well-rounded and effective writing program. Additionally, it is important to provide clear instructions, guidance, and feedback for each task to help L2 writers improve their writing skills. More precisely, when it comes to effective writing tasks, the following examples provide guidance for teachers in creating well-organized writing exercises for L2 learners.

Developing Dictation and Dicto-comp Items

Dictation primarily assesses listening skills, as L2 learners write down what they hear aurally, making it an imitative type of writing. In dictation, the teacher reads a passage aloud, and the students must write down exactly what they hear. It assesses learners' listening comprehension, spelling, and ability to accurately transcribe spoken language. Correct spelling is crucial in dictation, and it involves inserting punctuation while listening to stretches of discourse, which can be considered a controlled or intensive form of writing.

A related controlled writing form is dicto-comp. In dicto-comp, a paragraph is read at normal speed, and L2 learners rewrite it from memory. The teacher reads a passage, but some words are omitted, and students must fill in the missing words. Sometimes, key words from the paragraph are provided as cues. Dicto-comp is classified as an intensive or responsive writing task since L2 learners internalize the passage, recall key phrases, and re-create the story in their own words. Both dictation and dicto-comp tasks effectively gauge L2 learners' listening comprehension and writing abilities.

Example

1. The teacher reads the following paragraph at normal speed:
   "Yesterday was a beautiful sunny day. I went to the park with my friends. We played frisbee and had a picnic. After that, we went for a walk and enjoyed the lovely weather."
2. After listening to the paragraph, the teacher asks the students to rewrite it from memory.
3. Alternatively, the teacher provides a handout with key words from the paragraph, such as:

▪ Yesterday	▪ Beautiful sunny day	▪ Park
▪ Friends	▪ Frisbee	▪ Picnic
▪ Walk	▪ Lovely weather	

4. The students use the key words as cues and re-create the paragraph in their own words based on their memory or using the provided key words.

Developing Grammatical Transformation Items

In this type of task, students are given a sentence, and they must rewrite it by changing the structure or form of the sentence while retaining the original meaning. It assesses learners' understanding of grammar rules and their ability to manipulate language.

Example

Original Sentence: She is going to the store.
Transformation: Change the sentence to a negative form.

(possible answer) She is not going to the store.

Activity: Editing Exercise (Correcting Grammar, Spelling, and Punctuation)

Read the following paragraph carefully. It contains several deliberate errors in grammar, spelling, and punctuation. Your task is to identify these errors and correct them. Pay close attention to verb tenses, subject-verb agreement, punctuation marks, spelling mistakes, and sentence structure. Write the corrected paragraph on a separate sheet of paper.

Original Paragraph with Errors:
Yesterday, I goes to the library to borrowed a book about the solar system, but I finds out it was close. The librarian, who's very helpful, told me that it will be open again on Monday. "Since you're hear," she

said, "Why don't you check out our online resources?" She show me how to access ebooks and articles from the library's website. I was amaze by the amount of information available. I ended up find a lot of useful material for my project. In the end, it was a productive day, despite the initial dissapointment.

Developing Picture-cued Task Items

Students are provided with a picture, and they must write a story, description, or dialogue based on the visual stimulus. It assesses students' creativity, descriptive skills, and ability to use context to generate content.

Picture description task: A picture description is a language assessment task designed to measure L2 writing ability. In this task, L2 writers are presented with a visual image or picture, and they are required to write a descriptive response based on the content of the picture. The main objective of this task is to evaluate the L2 learners' writing ability to effectively convey information, ideas, and emotions in written form using the target language.

Example

City Street Scene: Display a picture of a busy city street with various activities and people. Ask students to write a descriptive paragraph detailing what they see, the atmosphere, and any interesting events or interactions they notice.

Picture sequence description: A picture sequence description task in an L2 writing test is designed to measure L2 learners' writing ability to narrate a series of events or actions based on a set of related images. In this task, learners are presented with a sequence of pictures that depict a coherent story, process, or sequence of events. This task evaluates the L2 learners' language proficiency, storytelling skills, and ability to use appropriate vocabulary, grammar, and organization to convey information in written form.

Example

Making a Sandwich: Present a sequence of images showing the steps to make a sandwich. Students should write a clear and organized set of instructions, using appropriate transition words and imperative verbs.

tomato, butter, cheese, bread slice, spread

Developing Order Tasks

In order tasks, students are given a jumbled set of sentences, and they must arrange them in a logical sequence to form a coherent paragraph or story. It assesses students' understanding of logical organization and coherence in writing.

Example

Below are four jumbled sentences related to planning a picnic. Rearrange them in the correct order to form a well-structured paragraph.

We should also bring some games and outdoor activities to keep everyone entertained.

• It would be best to choose a scenic spot with enough shade and space for everyone.

- To make the picnic enjoyable, let's plan to bring a variety of delicious food and drinks.
- First, we need to decide on a suitable date and invite all our friends and family.

Instructions:

Rearrange the sentences in the correct order to form a coherent paragraph. Use appropriate transitional words or phrases to connect the sentences.

Standardized Tests of Writing Tasks

Standardized tests of writing, such as TOEFL and TOEIC, typically assess a test-taker's ability to communicate effectively in written English. These tests consist of individual writing tasks and integrated tasks, each serving different purposes to evaluate learners' writing skills.

TOEFL Writing Tasks

- **Individual Writing Task:** In the individual writing task, test-takers are presented with a specific prompt or topic and are required to produce a well-organized essay or response independently. They are expected to demonstrate their ability to generate ideas, structure their writing logically, use appropriate language, and convey their thoughts clearly. The essays are typically scored based on various criteria, such as coherence, grammar, vocabulary, and overall quality of the response.

Example

Prompt: Some people believe that the best way to learn a foreign language is to immerse oneself in the country where the language is spoken. Others argue that taking language courses in their home country is more effective. Which approach do you think is better? Use specific reasons and examples to support your opinion.

- **Integrated Writing Task**: In integrated writing tasks, test-takers are presented with a passage (often an academic or general topic) and a related audio recording (a lecture or conversation). They must then summarize the main points from both the reading and listening materials and demonstrate their ability to synthesize information. This task assesses their listening and note-taking skills, as well as their ability to organize and express the information effectively.

Example

Prompt: The reading passage discusses the decline of bee populations worldwide and its potential impact on agriculture. The audio recording explains various strategies being considered to address this issue. Summarize the main points from the reading and the lecture. Be sure to explain how the lecture challenges or supports the points made in the reading.

In this example, the test-taker needs to listen carefully to the audio recording and take notes on the key points while also recalling the main points from the reading. They then need to write a coherent summary that highlights the connections between the reading and the listening materials.

TOEIC Writing Tasks

The TOEIC test includes both opinion essay items and written request writing tasks to assess the test-taker's ability to communicate effectively in various real-life situations or job-related context.

- **Opinion Essay Task**: Opinion essay items in the TOEIC test evaluate the test-taker's ability to express and support their opinions on a given topic. They are presented with a prompt that requires them to take a position on an issue and provide reasons and examples to back up their stance. These tasks assess critical thinking, language proficiency, and the ability to construct a well-organized and persuasive argument.

Example

Topic: "Should companies allow employees to work remotely?"

Prompt: In an essay, express your opinion on whether companies should allow employees to work remotely. Provide reasons and examples to support your viewpoint.

- **Written Request Writing Tasks**: Written request writing tasks in the TOEIC test evaluate the test-taker's ability to write a formal or semi-formal letter or email to make a request in a job-related or daily life situation. They are required to clearly state their request and provide necessary details using appropriate language and tone.

Example

Read the email

To: Homeowner
From: Taryn Kent
Subject: Your home
Sent: January 7

Hello. I've been looking at the photo gallery of your online home buyer's ad. Congratulations on trying to sell your home without a real estate agent. It is difficult (we have done it twice) but is worth the effort if you find a reasonable buyer. My sister is interested in buying a home in your region. Your home could be ideal if you are willing to negotiate the price. Your asking price is about $10,000 above her budget. She also wants to live near an elementary school and a bus route. I'm not sure if your home is near these amenities. Could you let me know about these details? Most importantly, are you open to negotiation on the price? Please let me know when the house would be available for viewing.

Thank you.
Sincerely,
Taryn Kent

Directions: Respond to the email as if you are trying to sell your house privately. Answer the questions and provide at least TWO details about the neighborhood and ONE reason why you can or can't negotiate the price.

In both TOEFL and TOEIC writing tasks, it's essential for the test-taker to manage their time effectively, plan their responses, and demonstrate a clear understanding of the prompt or the given materials. The writing tasks aim to evaluate the test-takers' ability to communicate appropriately and accurately in written English, reflecting their language proficiency and academic or workplace readiness. Standardized writing tasks are designed to assess an L2 learner's writing ability to communicate effectively in English. These tasks aim to evaluate L2 learners' language proficiency, writing skills, and their capacity to express ideas, opinions, and information in written form. Standardized writing tests play a crucial role in language assessment as they provide objective and consistent evaluation of an L2 learner's writing ability, allowing for comparisons across different individuals and groups.

These writing tasks are effective in assessing different aspects of L2 learners' writing abilities. Dictation and dicto-comp measure listening comprehension and accurate transcription, grammatical transformation tasks assess grammar proficiency, picture-cued tasks evaluate creativity and descriptive skills, and order tasks test logical organization and coherence in writing. Standardized writing tasks are designed to assess the writing ability of L2 learners to communicate effectively in English. By incorporating a variety of task types, educators can gain a comprehensive understanding of L2 learners' writing proficiency and provide targeted feedback and instruction to support their language development.

EXERCISES

Match the following terms with the correct definitions. Terms may be used more than once.

1. micro skills	6. writing ability
2. writing genres	7. descriptive writing
3. dicto-comp tasks	8. argumentative writing
4. order tasks	9. picture-cued tasks
5. writing strategies	

1. ___________ encompasses the skill to effectively convey written ideas and information in a clear and organized manner.

2. An ___________ is a piece of writing that aims to persuade the reader by presenting arguments and supporting evidence.

3. ___________ skills involve the fine details of writing, such as spelling, punctuation, and sentence structure.

4. ___________ involve techniques and approaches that writers use to plan, draft, revise, and edit their work.

5. In ___________, learners generate written responses based on visual cues or prompts.

6. ___________ skills encompass broader aspects like organization, coherence, and overall message.

7. ___________ require learners to arrange a set of jumbled sentences into a coherent paragraph.

8. Effective preparation for standardized writing tests involves practicing various ___________ and time management strategies.

9. ___________ combine dictation and composition, where learners transcribe a spoken passage and then expand it into a complete text.

UNIT 12.

Assessing Grammar and Vocabulary

Key Points

In this unit you will be able to:

1. Define the grammatical and vocabulary knowledge
2. Understand the nature of grammar and vocabulary ability in L2
3. Create effective vocabulary and grammar tasks for L2 readers
4. State the relationship between vocabulary and reading, and between vocabulary and writing in L2 educational context

Introduction to Assessing L2 Learners' Grammar and Vocabulary

Unit 12 centers on the critical components of language learning and assessment grammar and vocabulary. It underscores the importance of grammatical knowledge, encompassing rules, structures, and patterns essential for coherent and meaningful communication. The unit transitions from traditional paradigms focused on rote memorization to contemporary approaches that emphasize communicative competence, highlighting the need for assessment methods that evaluate both knowledge and application.

Assessing Grammar

- **Focus on Application**: Modern assessments prioritize learners' ability to use grammatical structures in real-world contexts, moving beyond mere rule recitation.

- **Integrated Skills**: Grammar assessment is increasingly embedded within tasks that require the integration of multiple language skills, reflecting authentic language use.

Assessing Vocabulary

- **Depth and Breadth**: Vocabulary assessments evaluate not only the range of words learners know but also their understanding of word meanings, usage, and collocations.
- **Contextual Understanding**: Emphasizes assessing vocabulary in context, gauging learners' ability to apply vocabulary knowledge in communication effectively.

Assessing L2 Learners' Grammar Ability

Grammatical knowledge refers to a language learner's understanding of the rules, structures, and patterns that govern the use of words and sentences in a particular language. It encompasses a range of elements, such as verb conjugations, noun declensions, sentence structure, word order, tenses, agreement, and more. This knowledge is crucial for forming coherent and meaningful communication in the language. In traditional language teaching paradigms, grammatical knowledge was often seen as the primary focus of language learning. Learners were expected to memorize rules, verb forms, and grammatical terminology, and language assessment tests would evaluate their ability to recall and reproduce these rules in isolation. However, with the emergence of communicative language teaching approaches, the focus shifted towards using language for meaningful communication in real-world situations. The goal became to help learners acquire not only grammatical competence but also functional and pragmatic abilities in the target language. In this context, grammatical knowledge is still regarded as vital, but it is integrated into the broader framework of effective communication.

Assessing a learner's grammatical competence has also evolved over time. Instead of testing learners' ability to memorize grammatical rules in isolation, assessments now emphasize how learners apply their grammatical knowledge in real-life language use. Language learners are evaluated based on their ability to comprehend and produce grammatically accurate and appropriate language during listening, speaking, reading, and writing tasks. By assessing grammar in context, it provides a more comprehensive understanding of a learner's language proficiency. In real-life communication, people rarely use language in isolated grammatical exercises; they use it to convey meaning and interact with others. Therefore, effective language assessment should reflect this real-world application of grammatical knowledge. In summary, grammatical knowledge remains a crucial aspect of language use, but its assessment has evolved to align with communicative language teaching principles. The focus is now on how learners can effectively apply their understanding of grammar to communicate meaningfully in various language contexts.

From the previous chapter, we discussed the communicative competence model proposed by Canale and Swain (1980), which consists of four components: grammatical competence, sociolinguistic competence, discourse competence, and strategic competence. In this model, grammatical competence is one of the key components, but the model does not explicitly illustrate how the different aspects of grammatical competence (phonology, lexis, syntax, and semantics) are associated with each other

(Brown & Abeywickrama, 2019). The conceptualization of grammatical knowledge by Larsen-Freeman (1991, 1997, 2003) consists of three interconnected elements: grammatical forms, grammatical meanings, and pragmatic meaning or use in a given context. These elements are critical for understanding how grammar operates in real-life communication. Here's a breakdown of each element:

- **Grammatical forms:** Grammatical forms refer to the structures of a language, encompassing both morphology and syntax. Morphology deals with how words are formed, including inflections, prefixes, suffixes, and word roots. Syntax, on the other hand, focuses on how words are combined to form sentences and phrases, including word order, sentence structure, and grammatical agreements. The accuracy of using grammatical forms is important for clear and effective communication.
- **Grammatical meanings:** Grammatical meanings involve both the literal and intended messages conveyed by the grammatical forms. It goes beyond understanding the surface-level structure of sentences and delves into the nuances of meaning conveyed by different grammatical choices. For example, different verb tenses can indicate actions that happened in the past, present, or future, and the choice of a particular tense can alter the meaning of a sentence significantly.
- **Pragmatic meaning or use in context:** Pragmatic meaning refers to the implied meaning that arises from the appropriate language choices a learner makes during a given communicative event. It involves understanding the sociolinguistic, sociocultural, psychological, and rhetorical aspects of a given context to use language appropriately. Pragmatic competence allows learners to adapt their language usage based on the situation, relationship with the interlocutor, and cultural norms.

Assessing grammatical knowledge involves targeting one or more of these elements of form and meaning. Purpura (2004) provided a taxonomy of components of grammatical knowledge, which can serve as a helpful guide for defining the construct of grammatical knowledge. This taxonomy can be used as a checklist of points to consider in form-focused assessments. Purpura's framework helps educators and language testers to break down grammatical knowledge into specific components, making it easier to design targeted assessments and identify learners' strengths and areas for improvement. By assessing different aspects of grammatical knowledge, educators can gain a comprehensive understanding of a learner's language proficiency and provide more tailored instruction to support their language development.

How to Design an Effective Grammar Task for L2 Learners

Now we explore various types of tests that can be utilized to measure grammatical knowledge in the classroom setting: multiple-choice, discrimination tasks, noticing tasks, gap-filling tasks, short-answer tasks.

Developing Multiple-choice Items

Multiple-choice tasks present L2 learners with a question or an incomplete sentence, and they must choose the correct answer from a set of options. These tasks are effective for testing discrete grammar points and can cover a wide range of language elements, such as verb forms, tenses, articles, prepositions, and more. Multiple-choice tasks are relatively easy to score and can efficiently assess learners' knowledge of specific grammar rules and forms or grammatical meaning.

Example

Grammatical form

Mina : What did you do yesterday?

Tony: I __________ to the park with my sister.

a) go b) went c) going d) goes

Grammatical meaning

Hani: Do you have any plan over the weekend?

James: I haven't decided yet. __________

Hani: Thanks, but I have to study for a math test next Monday.

a) How about you?

b) Need any help?

c) How about going hiking?

d) Need to work?

Developing Discrimination Items

Discrimination items are used to assess learners' ability to distinguish between two closely related areas of grammatical knowledge. Learners are presented with pairs of sentences or phrases, and they must identify which one is grammatically accurate based on specific grammar rules.

Example

Which sentence is correct?

a) She don't like ice cream.

b) She doesn't like ice cream.

Correct Answer: b) She doesn't like ice cream.

Developing Noticing Items

Noticing test items aim to develop L2 learners' awareness of specific grammatical features within a given context. Learners may be asked to identify and analyze grammar structures in a text, a dialogue, or a set of sentences. By consciously attending to form and/or meaning, learners develop an awareness of specific language features in English (Ellis, 1997, 2002, 2016). In these types of tasks, learners are encouraged to pay close attention to language patterns or particular language features in the given sample. In this noticing task, learners are presented with a passage containing several grammatical errors related to verb tense, subject-verb agreement, and verb form. It helps assess their ability to notice and correct grammatical errors, thereby indicating their understanding of grammar rules and usage in the target language.

Example

Instructions: Read the following passage and identify any grammatical errors you notice. Underline the error and write the correction above it.

Passage:

Last week, I have go to the grocery store to buying some fruits and vegetables. While I was there, I sees my friend Lisa. She tells me that she is going to the beach this weekend. I have never been to that beach, so I asks her if I can come along. Lisa agrees, and we plans to meet on Saturday morning.

Developing Fill-in-the-blanks Items

Gap-filling tasks involve providing learners with a sentence or a text with missing words or phrases. Learners must fill in the gaps with the appropriate grammatical elements, such as verbs, articles, or prepositions. These tasks assess learners' ability to apply grammar rules in context and produce accurate and meaningful language. In this gap-filling task, learners are provided with a passage with missing words. Their task is to select the appropriate words from the word bank and fill in the gaps to complete the passage. This task assesses learners' understanding of verb forms (present, past, and present perfect tenses) and subject-verb agreement, as well as their ability to use the correct verb forms in context. It requires both grammatical knowledge and comprehension of the overall meaning of the passage.

Example

Instructions: Complete the following passage by filling in the gaps with the appropriate words from the given word bank.

[Word Bank] is, are, have, has, was, were, been

Last summer, I __________ (1) fortunate enough to visit a beautiful island. The weather __________ (2) perfect, and the beaches __________ (3) breathtaking. During my stay, I __________ (4) many wonderful memories and experiences. One day, I __________ (5) snorkeling in the crystal-clear waters, and I __________ (6) able to see colorful fish and coral reefs. On another day, there __________ (7) a traditional festival, and the locals __________

(8) very welcoming and friendly. By the end of the trip, I ___________ (9) completely mesmerized by the islan's charm and beauty.

These different types of grammar assessment tasks offer various ways to evaluate learners' grammatical competence and proficiency. They can be used individually or in combination to provide a comprehensive understanding of learners' language abilities and to tailor instruction based on their specific needs and areas for improvement.

Activity: Sentence Reconstruction Exercise

Below are several sentences with their words in a jumbled order. Your task is to rearrange the words to form sentences that are both grammatically correct and logically coherent. Pay attention to the placement of subjects, verbs, adjectives, and any other parts of speech that might affect the sentence's clarity and correctness.

Jumbled Sentences:

1. the / library / returned / I / to / books / the
2. beautiful / in / garden / the / flowers / are / blooming
3. homework / finish / tonight / my / I / will
4. the / a / in / lives / small / village / old / man
5. delicious / cake / the / made / my / mother / is

Assessing L2 Learners' Vocabulary Ability

Words serve as the fundamental building blocks of language, enabling us to construct sentences, paragraphs, and complete texts. Native speakers effortlessly acquire vocabulary during childhood, with ongoing development as they encounter new experiences and concepts. However, for L2 learners, this process is more demanding and may require conscious effort. Some L2 learners deliberately expand their vocabulary by memorizing word lists or using bilingual dictionaries to bridge knowledge gaps (Brown & Abeywickrama, 2019). Vocabulary knowledge plays a pivotal role in achieving overall proficiency in an L2. It is essential for comprehension, communication, and expressing ideas effectively. As a result, it becomes imperative for language educators to actively explore and implement effective methods for both teaching and assessing vocabulary.

Effective vocabulary teaching strategies involve providing meaningful and contextualized exposure to words, using various techniques like visual aids, mnemonics, and vocabulary games to enhance retention and understanding. Encouraging learners to use newly acquired vocabulary in real-life situations and communicative activities further reinforces their knowledge and usage. Similarly, when assessing vocabulary in the classroom, teachers should design tasks that reflect learners' abilities to comprehend and produce words in different contexts. Assessments should go beyond simple memorization and focus on the learners' capacity to use vocabulary in conversations, writing, and comprehension exercises. This helps ensure that learners develop practical and functional vocabulary skills that are applicable in various language situations. By actively exploring and implementing effective vocabulary teaching and assessment methods, teachers can empower learners to build a strong vocabulary foundation, leading to improved language proficiency and successful communication in the L2.

When discussing the nature of vocabulary, it is important to define vocabulary for testing purposes. We can distinguish between words as tokens and types. Tokens encompass all the words in a paragraph, while types only include words of different forms, excluding repetitions. Another aspect to consider is the differentiation between function words and content words. Function words, such as prepositions, articles, and conjunctions, are more related to the grammar of the language than vocabulary. They primarily demonstrate associations among content words in sentences while content words consist of nouns, verbs, adjectives, and adverbs. Vocabulary tests generally focus on assessing learners' knowledge of content words.

In some cases, vocabulary tests might also examine larger lexical items, such as phrasal verbs (e.g., show up, come up with), compound nouns (e.g., blackboard, toothpaste, fish tank), or idioms (e.g., Hit the nail on the head, cost an arm and a leg, let the cat out of the bag), which only carry meaning as whole units. These larger lexical items have received less attention in traditional vocabulary tests due to the preference for single-word test items, which are easier to identify and score from word lists and texts.

In contrast, larger lexical phrases can be more complex as they vary in grammatical form and serve specific functions in spoken and written discourse. Consequently, they are more challenging to identify and evaluate. Nevertheless, these larger lexical items can still be utilized in vocabulary testing, especially when integrated into embedded, comprehensive, and context-dependent vocabulary measures (Read, 2000). By considering these various aspects of vocabulary, we can develop more effective vocabulary tests that accurately assess learners' language proficiency and understanding of different word forms and usage.

How to Design an Effective Vocabulary Task for L2 Learners

Assessing vocabulary knowledge in the L2 classroom requires varied approaches to capture the different aspects of word knowledge. Here are some assessment techniques commonly used to evaluate learners' vocabulary proficiency:

Developing Receptive Vocabulary Tests

Receptive vocabulary tests can be administered to test learners' understanding of newly introduced words. These quizzes may include matching exercises, or multiple-choice questions.

Example

Matching Exercise

Instructions: Match the words on the left with their corresponding definitions on the right.

Word List	Definitions
1) Eager	a) To delay or put off doing something.
2) Baffle	b) Feeling excited and passionate about something.
3) Procrastinate	c) To cause someone to be puzzled or confused.
4) Enthusiastic	d) Feeling impatient and enthusiastic to do or experience something.
5) Confused	e) Unable to understand or make sense of something.

Multiple-Choice Questions:
Instructions: Choose the correct synonym for the given word.

Expand:
a) Reduce
b) Increase
c) Shrink
d) Diminish

Developing Productive Vocabulary Tests

Productive vocabulary tasks involve recalling and using words in meaningful contexts or situations. One common type of vocabulary test is sentence completion, where the test-taker must understand the context of a sentence and provide the missing vocabulary item. To assess vocabulary knowledge more comprehensively, longer passages can be used to evaluate other aspects of vocabulary. In addition to word meaning, the form and usage of a lexical item can be examined. The selective deletion cloze or gap-fill test is an example of a test that incorporates these aspects of word knowledge. In this type of test, certain words are removed from the passage, and the test-taker must fill in the gaps with the appropriate vocabulary items, considering both their meaning and grammatical fit within the context. This productive testing type allows for a more thorough assessment of vocabulary knowledge and its practical application. In this gap-filling or selective deletion cloze test, the test-taker must identify not only the meaning but also the form of the lexical item required to fill in the blank.

Example

Fill-in-the-Blank Task

Instructions: Fill in the blanks with the appropriate words from the word bank.

[Word Bank] ambitious, confident, diligent, committed

She is a very ___________ student and always puts in the effort to achieve her goals.

Cloze Test

Instructions: In the following passage, some words have been removed. Fill in the gaps with the appropriate vocabulary words.

Language learning is an exciting journey that requires ___________ and dedication. When learning a new language, it's essential to ___________ a strong vocabulary foundation. Vocabulary forms the basis of communication, allowing learners to express their thoughts and ideas effectively. ___________ is an integral part of vocabulary acquisition. It involves actively using newly learned words in ___________ settings. For example, engaging in conversations, writing essays, or reading articles can help reinforce the ___________ of vocabulary words. To build a robust vocabulary, learners should regularly practice ___________ new words in various contexts. Flashcards, vocabulary quizzes, and ___________ exercises are effective techniques to aid memorization. Additionally, ___________ learning platforms and language exchange opportunities offer practical ways to expand one's lexicon.

Original Text:

Language learning is an exciting journey that requires **perseverance** and dedication. When learning a new language, it's essential to **establish** a strong vocabulary foundation. Vocabulary forms the basis of communication, allowing learners to express their thoughts and ideas effectively. **Practice** is an integral part of vocabulary acquisition. It involves actively using newly learned words in **authentic** settings. For example, engaging in conversations, writing essays, or reading articles can help reinforce the **retention** of vocabulary words. To build a robust vocabulary, learners should regularly practice **incorporating** new words in various contexts. Flashcards, vocabulary quizzes, and **cloze** exercises are effective techniques to aid memorization. Additionally, **digital** learning platforms and language exchange opportunities offer practical ways to expand one's lexicon.

Vocabulary Size Test

This test aims to measure a learner's vocabulary proficiency and the extent of their lexical knowledge. By quantifying the size of a learner's vocabulary, language educators and researchers can better understand the learner's language ability and identify areas for improvement. It involves presenting learners with a list of words and asking them to indicate which ones they know the meaning of. The purpose of a Vocabulary Size Test is to assess the number of words a person knows and recognizes in a specific language.

Example

1. see: They 〈saw it〉.
a) closed it tightly
b) waited for it
c) looked at it
d) started it up

2. time: They have a lot of 〈time〉.
a) money
b) food
c) hours
d) friends

Vocabulary Depth Test

This type of assessment examines the depth of learners' vocabulary knowledge by testing their ability to use words in different contexts, providing synonyms or antonyms, or asking for definitions and example sentences. In this word association test, test-takers need to select the words provided in the boxes (Read, 2000). While a Vocabulary Size Test focuses on the number of words a person knows, a Vocabulary Depth Test delves deeper into the learner's understanding and usage of those words.

Example

Instruction: There are eight words in the two boxes (left & right boxes). From the two boxes, select four words that you think are relevant to the stimulus word (i.e., 'sudden' in this example).

sudden:

beautiful quick surprising thirsty	change doctor noise school

By employing a combination of these assessment methods, language educators can gain a comprehensive understanding of learners' vocabulary knowledge, identify areas for improvement, and tailor instruction to support their vocabulary development in the L2 classroom.

Effective Strategies to Integrate Grammar and Vocabulary Knowledge

By integrating vocabulary and grammar knowledge in these ways, L2 language teachers can help learners to develop a deep and holistic understanding of the language, and to build the skills and confidence they need to use the language effectively in real-life situations. Integrating vocabulary knowledge and grammar knowledge in the L2 language classroom can be done by incorporating the following strategies:

- **Contextualizing vocabulary and grammar:** Teach vocabulary and grammar in the context of real-life situations, such as role-plays, simulations, and authentic materials. This helps learners to see the relevance of the language to their lives and provides a meaningful context for learning.

- **Scaffolding learning:** Provide appropriate support and guidance for learners as they work with new vocabulary and grammar structures. This can include explicit instruction, examples, and opportunities for practice.
- **Encouraging use of language:** Encourage learners to use vocabulary and grammar structures in meaningful ways, through speaking and writing activities, group work, and other interactive tasks. This helps learners to develop fluency and confidence in using the language.
- **Building connections:** Help learners to see connections between vocabulary and grammar, and between different aspects of language. For example, encourage them to think about how different vocabulary items relate to each other semantically, and how different grammar structures can be used to express similar ideas.
- **Using authentic materials:** Incorporate authentic materials, such as news articles, songs, and videos, into language instruction. These materials provide a rich source of vocabulary and grammar in context, and can help learners to see the real-life applications of language.
- **Monitoring progress:** Regularly assess and evaluate learner progress in vocabulary and grammar, and provide feedback that is focused, constructive, and specific. This helps learners to see where they are making progress and where they need to focus their efforts.

The Relationship between Vocabulary and Reading Comprehension

The relationship between vocabulary and reading comprehension is fundamental and tightly interconnected. Vocabulary knowledge is a crucial factor in determining an learner's reading comprehension ability, and the two skills often reinforce and support each other in the process of language development and understanding written texts. Specifically, vocabulary knowledge is instrumental in understanding the context of a given text. Many words have multiple meanings depending on the context in which they are used. A reader with a diverse vocabulary is more likely to recognize these nuances and infer the intended meaning of ambiguous words, improving overall comprehension. When engaged in reading, L2 learners draw upon their existing vocabulary knowledge to make inferences and connect ideas within the text. In this process, vocabulary plays a vital role in forming these connections and building a coherent mental representation of the information presented in the text. A rich vocabulary facilitates a deeper understanding of the relationships between words, sentences, and paragraphs, thereby leading to more profound comprehension.

Vocabulary serves as the building blocks of language comprehension. When a reader encounters unfamiliar words while reading, their understanding of the text can be hindered, as they may not grasp the intended meaning of those words and how they relate to the overall context. Consequently, a robust vocabulary repertoire allows readers to recognize and comprehend words quickly, making the reading process smoother and more efficient.

Moreover, In addition, efficient word recognition and decoding skills are essential for successful reading comprehension. A reader with a broad vocabulary can quickly recognize and understand familiar words, thereby enabling them to focus on the meaning of the text as a whole. On the other hand, readers with limited vocabulary may struggle to decode words, leading to a disjointed and less coherent comprehension process. In a Reading, in turn, contributes to vocabulary growth. As L2 learners encounter new words in various texts, they add these words to their lexicon and expand their vocabulary. The more they read, the more exposure they have to diverse vocabulary, enhancing their overall language skills and comprehension abilities.

In summary, vocabulary and reading comprehension are intimately intertwined in a symbiotic relationship. A strong vocabulary enhances reading comprehension by facilitating word recognition, supporting inferencing, and providing a solid foundation for understanding text context. Likewise, reading frequently and comprehensively exposes L2 learners to new vocabulary, leading to continuous language development and improved comprehension skills. As a result, educators and learners alike should recognize the significance of vocabulary acquisition as an essential component of successful reading comprehension.

The Relationship between Vocabulary and Writing Quality

Similarly, the relationship between vocabulary and writing quality also plays a critical role in determining the effectiveness and richness of a written product. Vocabulary serves as a fundamental element in shaping the clarity, precision, and overall impact of writing. A diverse and extensive vocabulary allows writers to express their ideas with greater precision and nuance. Using specific words and terms enables writers to convey their thoughts more accurately, leaving less room for ambiguity and ensuring that readers can comprehend the intended message more easily. A rich vocabulary contributes to the clarity and coherence of writing. When writers have access to a wide range of words, they can choose the most appropriate ones to convey their ideas. This choice of words enhances the flow of the text and ensures that the ideas are presented in a well-structured and organized manner, making it easier for readers to follow and understand. A robust vocabulary allows writers to avoid repetitive language and word usage. Repetition can diminish the quality of writing and make it less engaging for readers. By employing synonyms and varied expressions, writers can keep their writing fresh and engaging, holding the reader's interest throughout the text.

In descriptive writing, a rich vocabulary is particularly essential. Writers can paint vivid pictures and evoke emotions by employing descriptive language. The ability to use adjectives, adverbs, and figurative language enhances the sensory experience for readers and makes the writing more immersive and captivating. Vocabulary significantly influences the tone and style of writing. Different words and phrases convey different emotions and attitudes. By choosing words thoughtfully, writers can tailor the tone of their writing to suit the desired effect, whether it be formal, informal, persuasive, or narrative. In persuasive writing, a strong vocabulary can be a persuasive tool itself. Powerful and persuasive language can influence readers' opinions and attitudes, making the writing more impactful and effective in achieving its intended purpose. A varied vocabulary enables writers to engage their audience more effectively. By catering to the needs and preferences of different readers, writers can ensure that their message resonates with a broader range of readers. In summary, a well-developed vocabulary is a cornerstone of high-quality writing. It empowers writers to articulate their ideas clearly and concisely, maintain the interest of readers, and convey emotions and concepts with precision. Aspiring writers should continually work on expanding their vocabulary to improve the overall quality and impact of their written work.

Similarly, just as in the case of reading comprehension, the connection between vocabulary and the quality of writing plays a crucial role in determining how effective and rich a written piece is. Vocabulary stands as a key factor in shaping the clarity, precision, and overall impact of writing. An extensive and varied vocabulary offers writers the ability to express their thoughts more precisely and with subtlety. By selecting specific words and phrases, L2 writers can convey their ideas more accurately, reducing any uncertainty and ensuring that readers can grasp the intended message without difficulty.

Furthermore, a rich vocabulary contributes significantly to the coherence and organization of writing. When writers possess a wide array of words at their disposal, they can choose the most suitable ones to convey their concepts. This careful selection enhances the flow of the text, ensuring that ideas are presented in a logical and well-structured manner, ultimately making it easier for readers to follow and comprehend the content. Diversifying vocabulary usage also helps writers avoid repetitive language, which can negatively impact the quality of writing and diminish its engagement for readers. By incorporating synonyms and varying expressions, writers can infuse their work with freshness and maintain the reader's interest throughout the piece.

Vocabulary also greatly influences the tone and style of writing. Different words and phrases convey distinct emotions and attitudes. Through thoughtful word selection, writers can tailor the tone of their writing to match the desired effect, whether it's formal, informal, persuasive, or narrative.

In the context of descriptive writing, L2 writers can create vivid imagery and evoke emotions by incorporating descriptive language. The ability to incorporate adjectives, adverbs, and figurative language heightens the sensory experience for readers, immersing them in the writing and making it all the more captivating. Likewise, in persuasive writing, a strong vocabulary can serve as a persuasive tool in itself. Employing impactful and persuasive language has the potential to sway readers' opinions and attitudes, making the writing more effective in achieving its intended purpose. Thus, A well-developed vocabulary forms the foundation of high-quality writing. It empowers writers to articulate their ideas clearly and succinctly, sustain reader interest, and convey emotions and concepts with precision. Aspiring writers should consistently strive to expand their vocabulary in order to enhance the overall quality and impact of their written work.

EXERCISES

Match the following terms with the correct definitions. Terms may be used more than once.

1. micro grammar skills	8. vocabulary ability
2. receptive vocabulary tasks	9. micro vocabulary skills
3. macro grammar skills	10. productive vocabulary tasks
4. noticing items	11. discrimination items
5. metalinguistic	12. awareness
6. grammar ability	13. comprehension
7. matching words	

1. Identifying sentence fragments and correcting subject-verb agreement are examples of __________.
2. Crafting logical paragraph transitions and ensuring text flow fall under __________.
3. __________ involves the understanding and application of grammatical rules to construct coherent sentences.
4. Noticing tasks promote learners' __________ skills by drawing their attention to grammatical features in context.
5. The primary goal of discrimination and noticing tasks is to enhance learners' __________ of grammatical structures.
6. __________ refers to one's proficiency in understanding and using a diverse range of words in different contexts.
7. __________ involve understanding the meanings and nuances of individual words.

8. __________ encompass grasping the broader context of words within sentences and texts.

9. Developing __________ involves learning synonyms, antonyms, and the definitions of words.

10. __________ require learners to distinguish between similar grammatical forms and choose the correct one.

11. In __________, learners are prompted to identify specific errors or patterns within a given text.

12. __________ are crucial for determining the meaning of unfamiliar words based on their surrounding text.

13. The micro and macro vocabulary skills contribute to a learner's overall __________ of language.

14. In __________, learners identify the meanings of words when encountered in context.

15. __________ assess learners' ability to use words actively in sentences or dialogues.

16. __________ to their correct definitions is a common type of receptive vocabulary task.

17. In __________, learners may be required to write sentences that illustrate a target word's meaning.

References

Abeywickrama, P. (2019). *Exploring language assessment and testing: Reflections and practices*. Routledge.

Alderson, J. C., Clapham, C., & Wall, D. (1995). *Language test construction and evaluation*. Cambridge University Press.

Angelo, T. A., & Cross, K. P. (1993). *Classroom assessment techniques: A handbook for college teachers*. Jossey-Bass.

Armstrong, S., & Bailey, K. M. (1998). *Language testing and assessment: An advanced resource book*. Routledge.

Austin, J. L. (1962). *How to do things with words*. Oxford University Press.

Bachman, L. F., & Palmer, A. S. (2010). *Language assessment in practice*. Oxford University Press.

Bachman, L. F. (1990). *Fundamental considerations in language testing*. Oxford University Press.

Bachman, L. F. (2004). *Statistical analyses for language assessment*. Cambridge University Press.

Black, P., & Wiliam, D. (1998). Inside the black box: Raising standards through classroom assessment. *Phi Delta Kappan, 80*(2), 139-148.

Brown, H. D. (2004). *Language assessment: Principles and classroom practices*. Longman.

Brown, J. D. (2002). *The elements of language curriculum: A systematic approach to program development*. Heinle & Heinle.

Brown, H. D., & Abeywickrama, P. (2019). *Language assessment: Principles and classroom practices*. Pearson.

Brown, T., & Davis, S. (2018). The role of feedback in language instruction. In T. Green & S. Lee(Eds.), *New directions in language learning* (pp. 202-220). Language Press.

Canale, M. (1984). From communicative competence to communicative language pedagogy. *Language and Communication, 1*(1), 1-47.

Canale, M., & Swain, M. (1980). Theoretical bases of communicative approaches to second language teaching and testing. *Applied Linguistics, 1*(1), 1-47.

Cheng, L. (2008). *Washback, impact and consequences in language testing*. In E. Shohamy & N. H. Hornberger (Eds.), *Encyclopedia of Language and Education* (pp. 349-364). Springer.

Choi, I. (2008). The impact of EFL testing on EFL education in Korea. *Language Testing, 25*(1), 39-62.

Chomsky, N. (1957). *Syntactic structures*. Mouton.

Coombe, C., Folse, K., & Hubley, N. (2007). *A practical guide to assessing English language learners*. The University of Michigan Press.

Council of Europe. (2001). *Common European framework of reference for languages: Learning, teaching, assessment*. Cambridge University Press.

Davies, A. (2003). *The native speaker: Myth and reality*. Multilingual Matters.

Doe, J. (2020). Innovative methods in language teaching. *Journal of Language Teaching, 13*(4), 123-134. https://doi.org/10.1111/1234

Ebel, R. L. (1979). *Essentials of educational measurement*. Prentice-Hall.

Field, J. (2008). *Listening in the language classroom*. Cambridge University Press.

Goh, C. (2012). *Teaching and researching listening*. Routledge.

Greene, J. (2001). The role of task in the development of academic English. *ELT Journal, 55*(3), 255-265.

Gronlund, N. E. (2006). *Assessment of student achievement* (9th ed.). Allyn & Bacon.

Hallgren, K. A. (2012). Computing inter-rater reliability for observational data: An overview and tutorial. *Tutorials in Quantitative Methods for Psychology, 8*(1), 23-34.

Halliday, M. A. K. (1973). *Explorations in the functions of language*. Edward Arnold.

Hudson, T. (2000). *Test design: Developments in language assessment*. University of Hawaii Press.

Hughes, R. (1990). *Teaching and research: Options in grammar teaching*. Oxford University Press.

Hughes, A. (2004). *Testing for language Teachers* (2nd ed.). Cambridge University Press.

Jones, R. (2019). *Understanding digital literacies: A practical introduction*. Routledge.

Jonz, J. (1991). On the validity of reading assessments: A review of the literature. *Reading Research Quarterly, 26*(4), 371-383.

Jonz, J. (1994). Testing ESL composition: A practical approach. *TESOL Quarterly, 28*(4), 703-711.

Knoch, U. (2009). Diagnostic assessment of writing: A comparison of two rating scales. *Language Testing, 26*(2), 275-304.

Koyama, T. (2008). Assessing speaking in language exams: Issues and strategies. *Language Assessment Quarterly, 5*(3), 225-250.

Kunnan, A.J. (2004). *Test Fairness and Validation*. In M. Milanovic & C. Weir (Eds.), *European Language Testing in a Global Context* (pp. 27-48). British Council.

Lidz, C. S. (1991). *The language of children reared in poverty: Implications for evaluation and intervention*. Lawrence Erlbaum Associates.

Littlewood, W. (1981). *Communicative language teaching: An introduction*. Cambridge University Press.

Lynch, B. K. (2005). *Language program evaluation: Theory and practice*. Cambridge University Press.

Lynch, B. K., & Davidson, F. (1994). Criterion-refrenced language test development: Linking curricular, teachers, and tests. *TESOL Quarterly, 28*(4), 727-743.

May, L. (2011). Innovative approaches to reading assessment: An exploratory study. *Journal of Reading Behavior, 43*(1), 75-94.

McAlpine, J. (2002). *Placing English language education in a global context: Pitfalls and opportunities*. Routledge.

Messick, S. (1996). Validity of psychological assessment: Validation of inferences from persons' responses and performances as scientific inquiry into score meaning. *American Psychologist, 50*(9), 741-749.

Mousavi, S. A. (2002). *An introduction to applied linguistics: From practice to theory*. Edinburgh University Press.

Nakatsuhara, F. (2011). The effect of test-taker characteristics on performance in open-response listening tasks. *Applied Linguistics, 32*(2), 215-238.

Oller, J. W. (1979). *Language tests at school: A pragmatic approach*. Longman.

Oradee, T. (2012). Developing reading comprehension tests in ESL/EFL settings: A practical approach. *ELT Journal, 66*(3), 363-372.

Palmer, A. S. (2010). *Language assessment for classroom teachers*. Oxford University Press.

Plakans, L. (2013). *A history of language education in twentieth-century Australia and New Zealand*. Multilingual Matters.

Poehner, M. E., & Lantolf, J. P. (2005). *Dynamic assessment in the classroom: Vygotskian praxis for second language development*. Language Learning Monograph Series.

Purpura, J. E. (1999). *Learner strategy use and performance on language tests: A structural equation modeling approach*. Cambridge University Press.

Reinhardt, J. (2008). *Social Networking in Language Learning*. Palgrave Macmillan.

Rivers, W. M. (1981). *Teaching foreign-language skills*. University of Chicago Press.

Rost, M. (2014). *Teaching and researching listening* (3rd ed.). Pearson Education Limited.

Sadler, D. R. (2005). Interpretations of criteria-based assessment and Grading in Higher Education. *Assessment & Evaluation in Higher Education, 30*(2), 175-194.

Savignon, S. J. (1997). *Communicative competence: Theory and classroom practice*. McGraw-Hill.

Shohamy, E. (2001). *The power of tests: A critical perspective on the uses of language tests*. Longman.

Shrout, P. E., & Fleiss, J. L. (1979). Intraclass correlations: Uses in assessing rater reliability. *Psychological Bulletin, 86*(2), 420-428.

Skinner, B. F. (1957). *Verbal behavior*. Copley Publishing Group.

Smith, J. (2019). *Understanding language teaching: Techniques and methods*. Language Press.

Swain, M. (1980). Theoretical bases of communicative approaches to second language teaching and testing. *Applied Linguistics, 1*(1), 1-47.

Tafaghodtari, M. H. (2010). Enhancing listening comprehension skills through technology. *ELT Journal, 64*(4), 385-396.

Taylor, L. (2005). Washback and impact: ELT effects and impact. *ELT Journal, 59*(2), 154-158.

Taylor, C. S., & Nolen, S. B. (2008). *Classroom assessment: Supporting teaching and learning in real classrooms*. Pearson.

Vygotsky, L. S. (1978). *Mind in society: The development of higher psychological processes*. Harvard University Press.

Wajnryb, R. (1990). *Grammar dictation*. Oxford University Press.

Weigle, S. C. (2002). *Assessing writing*. Cambridge University Press.

Weir, C. J. (2005). *Language testing and validation: An evidence-based approach*. Palgrave Macmillan.

Weiss, C. H. (1972). *Evaluation research: Methods of assessing program effectiveness*. Prentice-Hall.

unit 1 Purpose of the Tests

Unit 1. Exercise Answers

1. aptitude test
2. assessment
3. diagnostic test
4. placement test
5. evaluation
6. proficiency
7. test
8. assessment
9. achievement
10. test
11. numbers
12. diagnostic
13. measurement
14. proficiency
15. achievement test
16. evaluation

unit 2 Types of Testing

Unit 2. Exercise Answers

1. alternative assessment
2. summative
3. dynamic assessment
4. criterion-referenced test
5. summative assessment
6. formative assessment
7. authentic
8. norm-referenced test
9. integrative testing
10. cloze test
11. alternative assessment
12. portfolio

unit 3 Quality of Assessment

Activity Identification of Potential Reliability Issues & Improvements

Rater Variability

- **Description**: Different raters might have varying levels of harshness or leniency, leading to inconsistent scoring across test administrations.
- **Improvement**: *Standardize rater training programs to calibrate scoring criteria and minimize subjective biases. Implement double-blind scoring where possible to ensure impartiality.*

Test Content Inconsistency

- **Description**: If the test content varies significantly from one version to another, it might not accurately measure the same language proficiency aspects consistently.
- **Improvement**: *Develop a comprehensive test specification that outlines specific skills, task types, and content areas to be assessed, ensuring that all test versions are equivalent in difficulty and scope.*

Test Administration Conditions

- **Description**: Fluctuations in test conditions, such as noise levels, technical issues with computer-based tests, or even the time of day, can impact students' performance.
- **Improvement**: *Standardize test administration procedures, including physical or digital testing environments, to provide a consistent testing experience. Regularly monitor and adjust conditions to ensure they meet predefined standards.*

Test-Taker Factors

- **Description**: External factors, such as test-taker's health, stress levels, or fatigue, can influence performance on test occasions differently.
- **Improvement**: *Provide clear guidelines for test-takers on preparing for the test, including recommended rest, and offer the option to reschedule if they experience adverse conditions on the test day.*

Question Ambiguity

- **Description**: Ambiguously phrased questions in a test can lead to misunderstandings, affecting test-takers' performance inconsistently.
- **Improvement**: *Review and revise test items regularly to ensure clarity and unambiguity. Conduct pilot testing with a sample of the target population to identify and correct problematic items before official administration.*

Unit 3. Exercise Answers

1. reliability
2. construct-related Validity
3. content-related validity
4. validity
5. variability
6. concurrent validity
7. washback effect
8. correlation
9. bias
10. predictive validity

unit 4 Test Specification

Unit 4. Exercise Answers

1. test specification
2. item types

3. purpose
4. elicitation
5. multiple-choice
6. scoring rubrics
7. test administration
8. content
9. validity

unit 5 Descriptive Statistics

Application Exercise Answers: Descriptive Statistics

1) a. Mean score for the Grammar test is 35.2.
   b. Standard deviation is 6.45.
   c. 100 students took the test.
2) a. The Total Proficiency Test has the highest possible score of 140.
   b. The Spelling test has the lowest possible score of 20.
3) a. No, all tests had the same number of participants (100).
   b. Since all tests had 100 participants, there's no difference in participation to discuss.
4) a. The Vocabulary test shows the greatest variability in scores, indicated by the highest standard deviation (12.30).
   b. The standard deviation is the highest for the Vocabulary test, indicating more score dispersion.
5) Additional information such as the detailed distribution of scores, median scores, and perhaps the range (maximum and minimum scores) would provide a clearer understanding of student performance and score dispersion.

Application Exercise Answers: Percentile Rank

1. Percentile rank for 90: 76.92%
2. Score corresponding to the 75th percentile: 85
3. Percentile rank for 82: 60%
4. Score corresponding to the 80th percentile: 90
5. Percentile rank for 75: 17.65%

Unit 5. Exercise Answers

1. central tendency
2. mode
3. descriptive statistics
4. positively skewed
5. range
6. nominal scales
7. mean
8. variance
9. negatively skewed
10. standard deviation
11. median
12. normal distribution

unit 6 Developing Scoring Criteria

Unit 6. Exercise Answers

1. item facility
2. primary-trait scoring
3. item discrimination
4. analytic scoring
5. holistic scoring
6. multiple-trait scoring
7. analytic scoring

unit 7 Teacher-made Criterion-referenced Tests and Standardized Norm-referenced Tests

Unit 7. Exercise Answers

1. feedback
2. norm-referenced test
3. evaluation criteria
4. norm-referenced test
5. criterion-referenced test
6. learning objectives

unit 8 Assessing Listening

Unit 8. Exercise Answers

1. gap-filling
2. proficiency
3. multiple-choice item
4. short response item

unit 9 Assessing Reading

Activity Developing Reading Comprehension Items

Main Idea

What is the passage primarily about?

A) The history of the Galápagos Islands

B) Charles Darwin's visit to the Galápagos Islands

C)* The unique biodiversity of the Islands and the challenges it faces

D) The impact of tourism on the Galápagos Islands

Detail

How far are the Galápagos Islands located from Ecuador?

A) About 500 kilometers
B)* About 1,000 kilometers
C) About 1,500 kilometers
D) About 2,000 kilometers

Detail

Which species is mentioned as being unique to the Galápagos Islands?

A) Koalas
B) Polar bears
C)* Giant Galápagos tortoises
D) Kangaroos

Inferential Understanding

Based on the passage, why are the Galápagos Islands considered a "living laboratory" for scientists?

A) Because of the diverse species that live in harmony
B) Because the islands are untouched by human influence
C)* Because of the unique adaptations of species
D) Because Charles Darwin developed his theory there

Inferential Understanding

What can be inferred about the challenges faced by the Galápagos Islands?

A) They are primarily due to natural disasters.
B)* They are related to tourism and climate change.
C) They are easily managed with current conservation efforts.
D) They are unrelated to human activities.

Unit 9. Exercise Answers

1. micro reading skills, macro reading skill
2. word-level
3. sentence
4. bottom-up
5. top-down
6. holistic
7. schema
8. top-down
9. interactive
10. metacognitive

unit 10 Assessing Speaking

Unit 10. Exercise Answers

1. intensive
2. micro skills/macro skills
3. responsive
4. speaking ability
5. interactive
6. intensive
7. responsive
8. interactive

unit 11 Assessing Writing

Activity Editing Exercise (Correcting Grammar, Spelling, and Punctuation)

1. Identify and correct the errors in the paragraph (Example Solution):

Yesterday, I **went** to the **library** to **borrow** a book about the solar system, but I **found** out it was **closed**. The librarian, who **is** very **helpful**, told me that it **would** be open again on Monday. "Since you're **here**," she said,

> "Why don't you check out our online resources?" She **showed** me how to access ebooks and articles from the **library's** website. I was **amazed** by the amount of **information** available. I ended up **finding** a lot of **useful** material for my project. In the end, it was a productive day, despite the initial **disappointment**.

This exercise not only tests learners' knowledge of English grammar and mechanics but also reinforces the importance of careful editing and proofreading in producing clear, error-free writing.

Unit 11. Exercise Answers

1. writing ability
2. argumentative writing
3. micro skills
4. writing strategies
5. picture-cued tasks
6. macro skills
7. order tasks
8. writing genres
9. dicto-comp tasks

unit 12 Assessing Grammar and Vocabulary

Activity Sentence Reconstruction Exercise

Reorder each jumbled group of words into a coherent sentence.

1. I returned the books to the library.
2. The flowers in the garden are blooming beautifully.

3. I will finish my homework tonight.
4. An old man lives in a small village.
5. The cake my mother made is delicious.

This exercise encourages active engagement with sentence construction rules, enhancing students' syntactic knowledge and their ability to form coherent statements, crucial for effective communication in English.

Unit 12. Exercise Answers

1. micro grammar skills
2. macro grammar skills
3. grammar ability
4. metalinguistic
5. awareness
6. vocabulary ability
7. micro vocabulary skills
8. macro vocabulary skills
9. micro vocabulary skills
10. discrimination items
11. noticing items
12. macro vocabulary skills
13. comprehension
14. receptive vocabulary tasks
15. productive vocabulary tasks
16. matching words
17. productive vocabulary tasks

저자와의
합의하에
인지를
생략합니다

A Practical Guide to Classroom-based Assessment in L2

지은이 신유선
펴낸이 조경희
펴낸곳 경문사
펴낸날 2024년 8월 1일 1판 1쇄
등 록 1979년 11월 9일 제1979-000023호
주 소 04057, 서울특별시 마포구 와우산로 174
전 화 (02)332-2004 팩스 (02)336-5193
이메일 kyungmoon@kyungmoon.com

값 21,000원

ISBN 979-11-6073-734-9